HARVARD ECONOMIC STUDIES

Volume CXIX

The studies in this series are published by the Department of Economics of Harvard University. The Department does not assume responsibility for the views expressed.

Oligopoly
and
Technical Progress

By

PAOLO SYLOS-LABINI

Translated from the Italian by
Elizabeth Henderson

HARVARD UNIVERSITY PRESS
Cambridge, Massachusetts
1 9 6 2

338.8
S98σ

Distributed in Great Britain by Oxford University Press, London

P.S.

Library of Congress Catalog Card Number: 62–13272
Printed in the United States of America

TO THE MEMORY OF
ALBERTO BREGLIA

Preface

This book was first published, in Italian (*Oligopolio e progresso tecnico*), in July 1956 in a provisional and small edition, copies of which I sent to my economist friends in Italy and abroad, asking them for their reactions. Exactly a year later a revised edition came out, in which, taking into account the comments and criticisms that had reached me, I made a number of changes (especially in the second and third parts), without, however, altering the structure of the book. In 1961 a third Italian edition was published.

Immediately after the appearance of the first edition, Harvard University Press published *Barriers to New Competition*, by Joe S. Bain, who, on the basis of a painstaking empirical investigation of American manufacturing, undertook a theoretical analysis of many of the same problems that occupied me in the first part of my book. In spite of the differences of approach in the two books, there is a striking resemblance in the results and conclusions—something of a rarity in the field of economic theory.

In the June 1958 issue of the *Journal of Political Economy*, Franco Modigliani published a paper, "New Developments on the Oligopoly Front," in which he worked out some of Bain's and my points mathematically. Considering the scientific value of Modigliani's analysis and the original approach to certain specific problems and their solution, his paper is to be regarded as more than a critical review of the two books; it is a new and significant contribution to the theoretical problem of oligopoly. Modigliani's article was followed by a long and interesting debate, which was published in the August 1959 issue of the *Journal of Political Economy*.

Two books published in 1959 — M. Shubik, *Strategy and Market Structure: Competition, Oligopoly, and the Theory of Games,* and W. J. Baumol, *Business Behavior, Value and Growth*

— deal with many of the same kind of problems as my own, but they use a different approach and reach different conclusions on several points. The differences are especially marked in the case of Baumol's work, although I believe them to be less important than might appear on first reading. The most recent contributions to the theory of oligopoly are discussed in two articles published in 1961: H. Mercillon, "Nouvelles orientations de la théorie de l'oligopole," *Revue d'économie politique,* no. 1 (1961), and M. Talamona, "Teoria dell'organizzazione, analisi microeconomica e teoria dell'oligopolio," *L'industria,* no. 2 (1961).

This edition of my book contains further revisions, again mostly in the second and even more so in the third part. But the structure is still the same as it was originally, no substantial alterations having been made. Nor have I attempted to work out the whole analysis anew in the light of Bain's and Modigliani's contributions, although I did try to make adjustments in the second and third parts to take account of some of Modigliani's criticisms. It seemed to me that if I were to recast my whole analysis, this would not only involve a radical revision of the logical structure of my book, but, just because of the kinship between my analysis and the two others mentioned, might also impair the homogeneous texture of my argument. Critical comparison, inferences, and perhaps integration are left to the reader. All I wish to add is that I make no claim whatever to priority.

The introduction discusses the question of modern industrial concentration from the historical and empirical point of view, with particular reference to the United States. Part One is concerned with the theoretical problem of price formation under oligopoly and uses what is called microeconomic analysis. The problems treated in Parts Two and Three are macroeconomic ones, which, given their greater complexity, are far more difficult to press into neat concepts and lend themselves less easily to theorizing. Today's economists feel a growing need to bridge the gap which has come to separate micro- and macroeconomics. It might be said that this book represents an attempt to find some common ground on which the two methods of analysis can meet and combine. Again, it is left to the reader to judge whether, and to what extent, I may have succeeded.

My acknowledgments for the critical comments I received after the 1956 edition are inserted at specific points throughout the book. It would, perhaps, have been simpler and more in accordance with common practice to say all my thank-yous here. I deliberately left them scattered in the text, first, in order to identify the changes made after 1956 and, secondly, to enliven the argument and to show it up for what, in large part, it is: the fruit of an interchange of views with many of my friends among economists.

In addition to those of my colleagues to whom I have expressed my thanks at various points and in addition to those who have reviewed the earlier editions, my gratitude is also due to Volrico Travaglini, Sergio Steve, Luigi Pasinetti, Gioacchino d'Ippolito, and Giacomo Becattini, who gave me the benefit of their views on the 1957 edition in personal conversation. While those named are not, of course, in any way responsible for errors in this book (and I should confess here that I did not always follow their advice), I am deeply in their debt for such improvements as this latest edition may be found to contain.

My very special thanks are due to Mrs. Elizabeth Henderson, the translator of this book. As anyone will know who has ever had the experience, translation of a work from one language into another is apt to bring to light much that is defective in form or weak in logic. In this particular case, the process of translation has proved uncommonly fruitful, thanks to the skill and experience (not to speak of the patience) of Mrs. Henderson, who for many years was Managing Editor of *International Economic Papers*. Her observations and suggestions have led me to introduce significant improvements not only of form but in some cases also of substance.

It was a great honor for me when this book was originally published in the series of the Department of Economics, University of Rome; now I am honored by seeing its translation into English appear as one of the Harvard Economic Studies.

University of Bologna   Paolo Sylos-Labini
September 1961

CONTENTS

Introduction: The Process of Industrial
Concentration and Market Forms   I

The origins of the process of industrial concentration — Statistical investigations — The relationship between concentration and market form — The modern analysis of market forms other than competition — The market power of large firms: recent critiques — Imperfect competition, differentiated oligopoly, and concentrated oligopoly — Conclusions.

Part One
OLIGOPOLY

I General Aspects of the Theoretical
Problem   19

The Hall-Hitch solution and marginal analysis — Direct cost and marginal cost — Comparison between the full-cost formula and the formula of marginal analysis.

II Price Determination   33

Outline of the proposed solution — Technological discontinuities — Criteria and assumptions of the model — Rate of profit, entry-preventing price, and elimination price — Long-run equilibrium in concentrated oligopoly — Some comments on the model — Oligopoly and competition — Differentiated oligopoly.

III Price and Cost Variations   57

The rationale of the full-cost principle — Variations in the determinants of equilibrium — Variations of direct cost and prices during prosperity — Variations of direct cost and prices during depression — Large firms and the prices of variable factors of production.

IV Marginal Analysis and Oligopoly   78

*The costing margin q and the elasticity of demand —
The validity of the marginalist principle — Profit maximization — The "degree of monopoly" and Kalecki's
theorem of the distribution of national income.*

V Profit and Wage Tendencies   89

*Unit profits — The question of overcapitalization —
Wage increases — Short-run price rigidity.*

Part Two
THE DISTRIBUTION OF THE
FRUITS OF TECHNICAL PROGRESS

VI The Mechanisms of Competition
and Oligopoly   103

*The classical theory — Comparison of the two mechan-
isms — Privileged firms — Privileged industries.*

VII Introduction of Machinery, Growth
of Income, and Level of Employment   112

*Ricardo on the introduction of machinery — Wicksell's
critique — A three-sector model — Alternative consequences of a cost reduction — Interpretation of the
analysis — Long-run price rigidity and economic policy.*

VIII The Creation and Reabsorption of Technological Unemployment   132

*Keynes and the relationship between investment and
employment — Labor-attracting and labor-repelling
forces — Keynes's equilibrium unemployment as a dynamic problem.*

IX Investment Opportunities
and Incentives   143

*Innovations, cost reductions, and expansion of demand
— Major innovations — The consequences of innovation
and Schumpeter's business-cycle theory — Innovations,
investment, and unemployment — Technical progress
and the large oligopolistic firm — The question of self-
financing — The process of concentration and the two
types of oligopoly.*

Part Three
EFFECTIVE DEMAND AND ECONOMIC STAGNATION

X The Problem of Effective Demand   159

*Demand and market form — The problem of excessive
saving — Investment, effective demand, and credit policy
— Spontaneous expansion of demand.*

XI Stagnation and Public Spending   170

*Hansen's theory — The multiplier and the degree of in-
dustrialization — The productivity of public expenditure
— Stagnation and public expenditure in the American
economy — American public expenditure in the postwar
period — Conclusion.*

Appendix   191

Works Cited   195

Index   203

Oligopoly and Technical Progress

Introduction: The Process of Industrial Concentration and Market Forms

It is the common view among students of economics that in the past competition ruled in industrial as in all other markets, and that it is only in our own age that market forms other than competition have become more and more frequent in the industries of advanced economies. The economist will be wise to acquaint himself with the works of economic historians, to see how much truth there is in this view.

Here is the account of Hermann Levy, a German scholar who has devoted his life to the study of the history of British and German industry:

The economic history of modern times shows that it was not individual competition which stood at the threshold of modern industrial capitalism. On the contrary, the early period of modern industrial capitalism was characterized by monopolies in many of the "new" trades, and by a capitalist domination over the guilds through some sort of putting-out system. This changed only with the emergence of factories. . . . The desire to "concentrate" disappeared and the competitive system took its place.

This changed, however, when from the eighties onwards a new revolution in markets set in, which was due to revolutionary progress in the means of transport and communication. . . . Industrial goods, and others too, could be produced wherever conditions of production were economically most favourable almost regardless of the cost of transport over long distances. This meant the possibility of concentrating production at certain points, of centralizing it where decentralization had previously prevailed, in order to supply concentrated markets, or drawing supplies from concentrated fields of production.[1]

[1] These somewhat bare statements are quoted from the concluding passages of *The New Industrial System* (London, 1936), pp. 270–1. Levy fully developed the argument not only in the same work, but also twenty-seven years earlier in *Monopole, Kartelle und Trusts,* published in English translation as *Monopoly and Competition* (London, 1911).

According to Levy, then, modern industry was initially marked by the prevalence of small monopolistic formations, many of which were grafted onto earlier systems of production. There followed a long period of competition (the first theorists of which were the classical economists), to be superseded in its turn by the recent phase of industrial concentration with its large and, in Levy's terminology, quasi-monopolistic industrial formations. The mainspring of the process was, basically, the quest for growing technical and economic efficiency. But the past and present forms of industrial concentration vary in different countries. Efficiency is not its only motive. Often policy interventions, especially of the protectionist variety, call forth monopolistic formations not necessarily connected with concentration. But side by side with these "artificial" monopolistic formations, there are others whose market power derives from structural changes in industry. At the same time, the policies which create or strengthen monopoly positions do not rest only on "theories," whether these be right or wrong; behind them there are usually powerful groups of interests, which cannot be dissociated from the process of concentration. The very fact that concentration goes on in so many different countries with different institutions and policies, and even in countries with ancient liberal traditions, proves that we are faced not with a series of fortuitous changes but with a structural process.[2]

If economic progress has led to concentration in many important industries, it has also created a great variety of small firms. However, these latter are often satellites of the big firms and cannot be considered on the same plane. More precisely, the modern process of concentration of firms pushes out of the market such small producers as make goods which have to compete with those made by the big firms, but the process is accompanied also by a mushrooming of small subsidiary and satellite enterprises, both in production and trade.

The origins of the process of industrial concentration

Hermann Levy is in many ways an original thinker. But, as far as the facts and the timing of the process of industrial con-

[2] See Levy, pp. 55–6, 273.

centration are concerned, he is at one with other economic historians. There is general agreement, in particular, to the effect that the process of concentration began to assert itself clearly from the 1870s on, although its origins, of course, lie further back.[3]

Why did this happen just then and not earlier? Levy says it was because of the revolution in the means of transport and communication. This reply, which he elaborated and discussed in detail in the more recent of the two works cited, gives the economist food for thought.

Modern means of transport obviously date much further back than 1870. But it was at about that time that their enormous development, and especially the spreading of railroads and steamships, made one market first of whole countries, then of continents, and ultimately of the world. Historically speaking, we may perhaps say that the principal source of competition and the agent of its continuous creation and re-creation for a long time was the reduction in transport costs and the ensuing disappearance of local barriers. Production units which enjoyed certain monopoly powers in limited areas gradually lost the natural protection of high transport costs; new firms were able to start up, and the strongest among the existing firms were able to expand and so to invade markets hitherto closed to them.

However, the very same process which destroyed local monopolies created — at first gradually and from a certain point on precipitately — more enduring monopolistic and oligopolistic positions, embracing whole countries.

Statistical investigations

In addition to occupying economists and economic historians, the process of industrial concentration has also engaged the attention of statisticians, especially in Great Britain and the United States.[4] Statistical investigations not only help us gain a better

[3] See, for example, J. H. Clapham, *An Economic History of Modern England*, III: *Machines and National Rivalries* (Cambridge, Eng., 1951), chap. 4; H. U. Faulkner, *American Economic History* (6th ed., New York, 1949), p. 436f.
[4] For Great Britain, see: H. Leak and A. Maizels, "The Structure of British Industry," *Journal of the Royal Statistical Society*, 1945, pp. 142–207; R. Evely and I. M. D. Little, *Concentration in British Industry* (Cambridge, Eng.,

knowledge of the quantitative aspect of the process, but they force us to define its content more rigorously. This is all to the good, considering how loosely the term "concentration" is often used.

For purposes of statistical research we have to make a three-fold distinction: concentration with reference to industrial plant (which we might call "technical concentration"), with reference to firms ("economic concentration"), and with reference to multi-product firms or groups of firms linked primarily by systems of interlocking finances and directorates ("financial concentration"). Generally speaking, we may take as a yardstick of concentration: (1) the number of workers employed; (2) the value of output; or (3) the value of assets. The first and second criteria — especially the first, which circumvents the problem of price changes — are relevant more particularly to technical and economic concentration; the third pertains more to financial concentration.

A high degree of technical and economic concentration in many industries creates the conditions of financial concentration not only within branches, but among several branches. Whatever form financial concentration may take, it always implies some sort of coordination of price and investment policies, and for this reason becomes especially interesting for the economist when it extends over related or complementary branches of production.

Furthermore, we have to distinguish between special concentration, related to some particular branch of industry or to some particular market, and general concentration, related to a broad sector of the economy (such as manufacturing industry).[5] The first concept is directly relevant to the study of market forms: the more concentrated a branch of industry, the less likely it is to operate in competitive conditions. The second concept is only indirectly relevant to the study of market forms: the higher the

---

1960). For the United States: W. L. Thorp and W. F. Crowder, *The Structure of Industry,* Temporary National Economic Committee, Monograph No. 27 (Washington, 1940); J. Steindl, *Small and Big Business* (Oxford, 1945), chap. 5; G. Rosenbluth, "Measures of Concentration," *Business Concentration and Price Policy,* National Bureau of Economic Research (New York, 1955), pp. 57–100.

[5] See E. S. Mason, *Economic Concentration and the Monopoly Problem* (Cambridge, Mass., 1957), pp. 16–43.

degree of general concentration, the more likely it is for horizontal and vertical integration and situations of price leadership to spread.

Various indices of concentration have been suggested, among them a concentration ratio in terms of the percentage of employment (or the value of output) in a fixed and limited number of firms (three, four, or five) as compared with the entire employment (or output) in a given branch of industry. Indices of this kind have an element of arbitrariness in the choice of the number of firms considered and are, furthermore, lopsided insofar as they are a very imperfect reflection of the real inequalities between the larger and the smaller production units (firms or establishments); yet these inequalities are important for the study of market forms,[6] as will be seen in the course of the analysis to be developed in this book. Gini's concentration ratio,[7] which is based on the Lorenz curve, is largely free of these defects: it takes account of the whole structure of the industry concerned and reflects at the same time the concentration and the inequality of production units. In any event, all measurements of concentration, including Gini's, give us no more than first and very rough indications for the study of market forms. An industry may not be highly concentrated at all and yet have noncompetitive conditions, if the products are differentiated or if the market is subdivided into many small local markets. Conversely, a highly concentrated industry need not necessarily have monopolistic or oligopolistic conditions, if its products are readily replaceable by others. In the larger view, one must also take account of the relative importance of different branches and their function in the

[6] This was formally recognized by Evely and Little (especially in chap. 2), who used a concentration ratio based on a fixed number of firms (three), but supplemented it by other indicators, in particular the size ratio of business units (average employment in the three largest units divided by average employment in the other units) and the size ratio of plants (average employment per establishment of the three largest units divided by average employment per establishment in the other units).

[7] C. Gini, "Sulla misura della concentrazione e della variabilità dei caratteri," *Atti del Reale Istituto Veneto di scienze, lettere ed arti,* LXXIII, part 2, pp. 1203–48. Note that Gini's concentration ratio may vary between 0 and 1. See also M. J. Bowman, "A Graphical Analysis of Personal Income Distribution," *Readings in the Theory of Income Distribution,* ed. W. Fellner and B. F. Haley (Philadelphia, 1946), pp. 72–99.

process of production: the steel industry cannot be considered on the same plane as the confectionery industry.

It follows that statistical investigations are merely a point of departure and can in no way replace qualitative case studies of particular branches of industry.[8] This is especially true for the study of financial concentration, where statistics are of very little use. The data for such investigations are difficult to obtain, especially as regards changes in concentration over a long period — here there is the additional difficulty of periodic changes in the classificatory definitions of industrial censuses. The most readily accessible data are those of the distribution of establishments according to the number of workers or, more generally, employees.

Fortunately, technical concentration in terms of the number of workers employed in separate branches of industry happens to be the type of concentration most relevant to our problem; both economic and financial concentration are largely conditioned by technical concentration and, while they may be highly relevant to other types of analysis, it is not essential to consider them here.

The appendix included at the end of this book contains some indices of concentration that I have calculated on various criteria and with Gini's method.[9] The comments are very brief, but the results confirm the majority view among economists: that industrial concentration is high in the United States and has been growing during recent decades.[10]

Some American scholars not long ago published figures tending to show (1) that the process of concentration in the United States practically came to a standstill about half a century ago, after having reached high levels as a result of the giant mergers at the end of the nineteenth and beginning of the twentieth century, and (2) that the "degree of monopoly" in the United States, while considerable, has remained almost unchanged since the beginning

---

[8] See Evely and Little, pp. 47–8.

[9] I have also included some data taken from an official United States publication, showing the share of value added accounted for by the largest companies in 1947 and 1954 (Appendix, III, 2).

[10] As we learn from economic history, the two periods when the process of industrial concentration in the United States was most marked were the years around the turn of the last century (especially from 1897 to 1903) and the years preceding the Great Depression (1924 to 1929).

of this century.[11] We need not discuss the second statement, although, in Chapter 4, we shall have more to say on the notion of degree of monopoly. The first statement is more interesting and would seem to contradict the view prevailing among economists, as well as the results of my own research. This view is propounded by M. A. Adelman.[12] He calls "industry concentration ratio" the percentage value of the output of a fixed and limited number of firms (four). He admits that "the industry concentration ratio, and all the others based on small numbers, suffers from the arbitrary element in the choice of numbers, and also wastes all the available information about the structure of the group itself." [13] But he then uses his ratio for long-period comparisons,[14] where it can become more misleading. However, Adelman's study is not without value. There is no contradiction between my findings on concentration with reference to the whole group of firms making up a given "industry" and Adelman's findings for a limited number of firms. It will become clear later in this study that the process of concentration relevant to market forms is that shown by a concentration index referring to all or most of the firms in a given "industry." But Adelman's results might suggest that this process is fully compatible with irregular variations, and not necessarily increases, in the relative share of the three or four largest firms.

The explanation (which concerns the economist rather than the statistician) may be this: some medium-sized or large, but not yet giant, firms grow either by internal expansion or, more often,[15] by merger with others and so enter the class of giant firms — which is, indeed, limited but not composed of a fixed number of firms. This sort of development has certainly taken place in the American iron and steel industry.[16] But once con-

[11] C. Warren Nutter, *The Extent of Enterprise Monopoly in the United States 1899-1939* (Chicago, 1951). We must point out that the concept of "degree of monopoly" proposed by Nutter seems arbitrary.

[12] "The Measurement of Industrial Concentration," *Review of Economics and Statistics*, no. 4 (1951).

[13] *Ibid.*, p. 271.

[14] *Ibid.*, p. 291.

[15] G. Stigler, "The Statistics of Monopoly and Merger," *Journal of Political Economy*, no. 1 (1956), p. 40.

[16] W. Adams, "The Steel Industry," *The Structure of American Industry*, ed. W. Adams (2nd ed., New York, 1954), p. 156.

centration has become very high in some branch of production, it is of little interest to the economist to know exactly whether it has increased or diminished. Whether there are still four giant firms, or three or five or six, makes no real difference in the situation and the market form. To all intents and purposes, the market has reached the limit of concentration.

To return to our own problem, Gini's ratio ceases to be relevant when the number of firms (or establishments) is very small — say, less than ten or fifteen. But then the structure of a given industry can be described, in empirical and economic terms, without the help of an index of concentration. Empirically, it is enough to say how many units there are and how large each of them is. From the point of view of economics, the industry is obviously oligopolistic. The industry can also be said to be "concentrated." This case of a small number of firms may be described as "absolute concentration," to distinguish it from the above case of "relative concentration" where there are many firms and a few dominating ones.

The relationship between concentration and market form

What relationship is there between the process of industrial concentration and market form? The answer is: the process of industrial concentration generates or increases the largest firms' market power. There are a number of explanations for this.

Let us recall an observation made long ago by Adam Smith: when the number of entrepreneurs is small, or has become so, they can easily agree among themselves to regulate prices.[17] This has to be qualified by stating that the process of concentration must be far advanced, because only then can it be assumed that a few large firms are in a position to control a sizable part of output. The qualification is more significant than the main assertion; it puts us on guard against identifying or confusing the processes of concentration and monopolization. The first does not necessarily imply the second.[18]

---

[17] *Wealth of Nations,* Book I, chap. 8.

[18] It seems that in the agricultural economy of the most advanced countries, or at any rate of the United States, medium-sized farms have become larger and there has even been some concentration of farms. Neither tendency is

It has also been noted that, in many branches of industry, modern techniques gradually have caused an increase, in absolute and relative terms, of the minimum capital required to organize production at sufficiently low cost. This creates a "natural" obstacle to competition. This observation, which was in substance made by Marx,[19] is open to an objection. While it is true that in many, and probably in most, industries minimum capital requirements have grown, it is equally true that, thanks to the development of stock exchanges and banking, the possibilities of obtaining funds have also grown. It is by no means excluded that today's larger capital requirements may be matched by the larger potential of the credit system, and the consequences for market forms remain doubtful, to say the least. This objection is not decisive. It is common knowledge that very large and well-established firms find it much easier to obtain loans or otherwise to dispose of funds than do small, medium-sized, or new firms. It is precisely this which creates an obstacle to competition. Nevertheless, the objection does retain some weight.

It is perfectly reasonable to assume that, in contrast with pure competition, changes in the output of giant firms in concentrated industries do influence prices, and it is often thought that this entitles us to draw on the theory of oligopoly. But, as we shall see, the theory of oligopoly is in a fluid, not to say chaotic, state. In consequence, the problem of the market power of giant firms in concentrated industries remains to be solved.

All in all, the analysis of the relationship between the process of concentration and market form is in a completely unsatisfactory state — in blatant contrast with the analysis of market forms other than competition which have no necessary connection to the process of concentration or even preclude it in certain cases (such as retail trade). Paradoxically, the modern economist's theoretical "toolbox" makes it easier for him to conduct a rigor-

---

definitely clear, especially the latter. (See "The Future of the Small Farm — A Symposium," *Contemporary Readings in Agricultural Economics*, ed. H. C. Halcrow, New York, 1955, p. 77f.) But even if such processes did take place, they did not — apart from public intervention — lead to monopolization, precisely because in agriculture concentration is very far from the high levels necessary to give real market power to the largest firms.

[19] *Capital*, Book I, chap. 23, pgh. 2.

ous analysis of the economic consequences of the market power enjoyed by suppliers, who are to be considered tiny monopolists in their own sphere, than to conduct an equally rigorous analysis of the economic consequences of United States Steel Corporation's market power.

Let us see how this situation came about.

The modern analysis of market forms other than competition

When Piero Sraffa published his famous critique of Marshallian theory, the situation was, in a certain sense, the opposite. Everybody, including Marshall himself, took it for granted that the trusts and giant firms in highly concentrated industries were in some way monopolistic. The problem seemed to invite historical and empirical research rather than refined theoretical analysis. Economists actually deduced the prevailing market form in a given branch of industry from the number of firms in it, and, depending on whether there were relatively few or relatively many firms, the market form was described as approaching monopoly or approaching competition.

This is where Sraffa's critique set in. What was new and important in it was his demolishing of the notion that

when production is in the hands of a large number of concerns entirely independent of one another as regards control, the conclusions proper to competition may be applied even if the market in which the goods are exchanged is not absolutely perfect, for its imperfections are in general constituted by frictions which may simply retard or slightly modify the effects of the active forces of competition, but which the latter ultimately succeed in substantially overcoming. This view appears to be fundamentally inadmissible. Many of the obstacles which break up that unity of the market which is the essential condition of competition are not of the nature of "frictions," but are themselves active forces which produce permanent and even cumulative effects. They are frequently, moreover, endowed with sufficient stability to enable them to be made the subject of analysis based on statical assumptions.[20]

The overall, or social, effect of a multitude of very small monopolistic formations may well be greater, and indeed much greater, than that of enormous and immediately obvious monop-

[20] "The Laws of Returns under Competitive Conditions," *Economic Journal,* December 1926, p. 542.

olistic formations. Many economists realized at once that this view was true and important and deserved the most careful further study. But, overintent on analyzing what was not obvious and what it had been Sraffa's merit to make clear, they ended by neglecting to analyze the obvious: namely, the market power of very large industrial concerns. This is why, apart from the rather elementary observations of Smith and Marx, we are still in need of a really satisfactory theoretical analysis.

It is high time to analyze the obvious.

The market power of large firms: recent critiques

The weakness or downright inconsistency of the theoretical analysis of the market power of giant firms became apparent when certain economists attacked the widespread idea that such firms have monopolistic power just because they are so large. These economists turned Sraffa's argument upside down, as it were: if it is true that the presence of many firms in a given branch establishes neither the proof nor even the presumption of competition, the reverse is equally true; the presence of only a few firms does not mean that they must have monopoly powers. In such a situation it must be, and is, recognized that each separate firm's output has an appreciable influence on price and, hence, that there is no pure competition. But, so runs the argument, the concept of pure competition is a highly abstract one and is in any case applicable only to static conditions. What ultimately counts is the result; and from a dynamic point of view the result may be the same as, or even "better" than, that attributed to pure competition. If necessary, the concept of competition will have to be redefined in a more realistic manner, but in any event there is no point in repeating uncritically that large industrial concerns have monopoly powers.[21]

In embryonic form, a critical attitude of the same kind can be found in certain qualifications that Marshall introduced with respect to the monopoly power of trusts:

[21] The argument sketched out above was propounded by Joseph A. Schumpeter (*Capitalism, Socialism, and Democracy,* New York, 1947, chaps. 7 and 8) and by J. M. Clark ("Toward a Concept of Workable Competition," *American Economic Review,* June 1940).

It is true that when nearly the whole of any branch of industry is in the hands of a few giant businesses, none of them can be fairly described as "representative." If these businesses are fused in a trust, or even closely combined with one another, the term "normal expenses of production" ceases to have a precise meaning. And, as will be argued fully in a later volume, it must be regarded as *prima facie* a monopoly; and its procedure must be analysed on the lines of Book V, Chapter XIV ("The theory of monopolies"); though the last years of the nineteenth century and the early years of this have shown that even in such cases competition has a much greater force, and the use of the term "normal" is less inappropriate than seemed probable *a priori.*[22]

These qualifications are vague and contradictory. What is black *prima facie* and *a priori* becomes white *a posteriori*. Some modern economists have been more consistent and have called it white all along.

Imperfect competition, differentiated oligopoly, and concentrated oligopoly

There are, then, two distinct problems. One has to do with Sraffa's world of many small and apparently competing firms, which in fact have quite definite monopoly power. The other concerns the situation of industries producing fairly homogeneous (or not highly differentiated) goods in a concentrated branch, where a limited (and variable, but always small) number of firms controls the whole or the major part of production.

The first situation has been exhaustively analyzed by the theoreticians of imperfect and/or monopolistic competition. It most frequently occurs in trade and in the production of manufactured consumer goods, where products are as a rule differentiated with respect to the consumers. The concept of "industry," strictly speaking, loses its significance (Sraffa, Robinson) and the concept of "market" remains valid only if a distinction is made between the particular market for the products of each firm and the general market for these products together with directly substitutable ones.[23] The extent of the general market cannot be defined in absolute terms but depends on the substitutability or,

---

[22] Alfred Marshall, *Principles of Economics,* Appendix H. See also his *Industry and Trade,* Book III, chap. 1, pgh. 4.
[23] Sraffa, pp. 545–46.

more precisely, on the degree of crosselasticity of the demand under consideration.[24]

Nicholas Kaldor further specified, correctly, that "each seller is in close competition with only a few others; that these others are themselves in competition with a small number of different firms; and that chains of such oligopolistic groups compose the whole market." [25] Oligopoly is, in fact, he said, "the most common condition." Kaldor's observation is important. It suggests that the markets in which imperfect competition prevails are not entirely disconnected and that for purposes of theoretical analysis the relevant unit is not the single firm, but the group of firms competing directly — though imperfectly — with each other.[26] In short, his point implies that the theory of oligopoly represents, with respect to the theory of imperfect competition, a further approximation to reality. We shall describe this situation, in which there is always some product differentiation, as "differentiated oligopoly" or, perhaps more accurately, "imperfect oligopoly."

However, it is really the other situation, that of a highly concentrated industry, which needs more careful analysis. This is essentially the situation which John K. Galbraith had in mind when, recalling the conclusions of a number of empirical studies on the structure of American industry, he wrote that "oligopoly is the appropriate assumption in dealing with industrial markets in the United States." [27] We shall use the term "concentrated oligopoly" to describe such a situation.[28] Finally, there is an

[24] Cf. R. Triffin, Monopolistic Competition and General Equilibrium Theory (Cambridge, Mass., 1940).
[25] "Market Imperfection and Excess Capacity," Economica, March 1935, pp. 30–50; the quotations are taken from T. N. Wolfe's astute comments on Kaldor's ideas in "The Problem of Oligopoly," Review of Economic Studies, no. 56 (1953–54), p. 181.
[26] See also Edward H. Chamberlin, The Theory of Monopolistic Competition (5th ed., Cambridge, Mass., 1947), p. 81f.
[27] "Monopoly and the Concentration of Economic Power," A Survey of Contemporary Economics, ed. H. S. Ellis (Philadelphia, 1948), I, 107.
[28] C. Wilcox criticized Galbraith and Bain and denied the "ubiquity" of oligopoly ("On the Alleged Ubiquity of Oligopoly," American Economic Review, Supplement, March 1950). But on closer inspection Wilcox's argument will be seen to apply only to concentrated oligopoly, not to differentiated oligopoly. Wilcox himself admits that (concentrated) oligopoly is often found

intermediate situation, with the characteristics of both concentration and differentiation; we shall speak, in this case, of "mixed oligopoly."

Oligopoly, then, is not a special and abstract case; it is, in one shape or another, the most frequent market form of modern economies.

Conclusions

Before coming to the end of these introductory remarks, we must return for a moment to that common view which we recalled at the beginning and which is supported by distinguished economic historians — the view that in the past competition was the rule and that in the present other and essentially oligopolistic market forms tend to prevail.

This view needs some qualification. Monopolistic and oligopolistic forms have always existed, even in the golden age of competition. It is a question of degree. But there are also *new* market forms, and the question is: where do they exist? Not in agriculture, where competition is still the rule — or, better, would be the rule in the absence of government intervention. Nor do they occur in retail trade. As long ago as 1848 John Stuart Mill wrote:

> The wholesale trade, in the great articles of commerce, is really under the dominion of competition. . . . But retail price, the price paid by the actual consumer, seems to feel very slowly and imperfectly the effect of competition; and when competition does exist, it often, instead of lowering prices, merely divides the gains of a high price among a great number of dealers.[29]

And in 1901, Knut Wicksell expressed with perfect clarity some of the essential points of the modern theory of imperfect competition:

> We should not forget that practically every retailer possesses, within his immediate circle, what we may call an actual sales *monopoly*, even if, as we shall soon see, it is based only on the ignorance and lack of organ-

---

in the capital-goods industries — above all, we may add, in heavy industry. In its turn, differentiated oligopoly prevails in light industry and trade.

[29] *Principles of Political Economy,* Book II, chap. 4 ("Of Competition and Custom"), pgh. 3.

ization of the buyers. He cannot, of course, like a true monopolist, raise prices at will — only in places remote from trade centres can a considerable local rise in prices occur — but if he maintains the same prices and qualities as his competitors, he can almost always count upon his immediate neighbourhood for customers. The result is not infrequently an *excess of retailers,* apparently for the convenience, but really to the *injury, of the consumers.*" [30]

Wicksell went on to prove this proposition no less, and perhaps more, effectively than Joan Robinson and E. H. Chamberlin, who have since made us all familiar with it.

Thus we see that imperfect competition and differentiated oligopoly are rather old market forms in retail trade. The essential novelty, which enables us to distinguish two stages in the development of modern capitalism, is connected with the process of industrial concentration. Theoretically, the new market form is that of *concentrated oligopoly.*

This market form and the process which generates it are more especially peculiar to modern industry in highly developed countries; but a similar process is at work in the retail trade of mass consumption goods, thanks to the development of the great department and chain stores, which certainly have both more market power and more efficiency than the small shops. However, chronologically and logically, commercial concentration (in the technical and organizational sense) *follows* industrial concentration. Concerning market form, the new large commercial units can best be described as approximating concentrated oligopoly.

Part One of this book discusses the theoretical problem of oligopoly. We shall first consider the general aspects and then examine the two types of oligopoly that we have distinguished. The focus will be on the second type: concentrated oligopoly.

[30] *Lectures on Political Economy,* trans. from the Swedish by E. Classen and ed. with an introduction by Lionel Robbins (London, 1934), I, 87.

Part One

OLIGOPOLY

I

General Aspects
of the Theoretical Problem

The theory of oligopoly is in a fluid state. The most diverse solutions have been and are still being put forward, and to choose among them is not an easy task. If we accept their assumptions, most of these solutions are formally correct and, what is more, mutually compatible. This puts us in a more difficult position than if we had to choose among contradictory theories. We are still in the situation which Schumpeter, voicing a fairly general opinion, described by saying that "oligopoly divides up into very many cases, some of which are determinate while others are not." [1] The counsel of a "case-by-case" approach is characteristic of a highly unsatisfactory theoretical situation.

One method often used to put some sort of order into the galaxy of hypotheses and solutions is to start with the simplest case of oligopoly, duopoly, and to distinguish between Cournot-type and Edgeworth-type solutions. The former end up with the conclusion that price is determinate and equilibrium stable, the latter with the conclusion that price is not necessarily deter-minate nor equilibrium necessarily stable. Both types of solution rest on abstract hypotheses of an essentially psychological nature. More and more complicated assumptions have been made about "reaction curves" and "conjectural variations." [2] The production of such hypotheses and solutions has assumed alarming propor-tions; Stackelberg, one of those who were busy in this field,

[1] *Business Cycles* (New York, 1939), p. 60n.
[2] For a critical review of such assumptions, see C. Napoleoni, "Oligopolio," *Dizionario di economia politica* (Milan, 1956).

eventually made the discovery that "a disconcertingly large number of possible cases" was involved.[3]

The truth is that there is no stopping on the path of conjectural variations (*Cred' io ch'ei credette ch'io credesse*).[4] Solutions can be proliferated to infinity and the manufacture of such hypotheses and solutions can become a sort of profession. It is all remarkably like working out the chess problems in a weekly magazine (white to play and mate in three moves) or, on a higher plane, like writing a manual of chess strategy. The analogy is not formal only, nor — we hope — is it disrespectful. A good chess player is much to be admired.[5]

In contrast with this school of economists there is another that propounds a single, very simple and perfectly determinate, solution, based on the assumption of a kinked demand curve. It will be recalled that this solution was simultaneously and independently suggested in England by Hall and Hitch, after a painstaking empirical investigation at Oxford just before the last war, and in the United States by Sweezy, who reached it by deduction, although he made explicit reference to the explanations which businessmen themselves give of their behavior.[6]

We need not here discuss the theories of the first school of economists; this has been done well by others. But it may be useful to summarize briefly the results of Hall, Hitch, and Sweezy, for this will help us in our subsequent argument.

The Hall-Hitch solution and marginal analysis

Generally speaking, according to Hall and Hitch, each individual businessman faces a demand curve which has a kink at

[3] W. Fellner, *Competition among the Few* (New York, 1949), p. 100.
[4] "I believe that he believed that I believed." Dante, *Inferno*, Canto XIII, 25.
[5] So, rightly, is a great mathematician. It is not by accident that the name of von Neumann should come to mind.
[6] R. L. Hall and C. J. Hitch, "Price Theory and Economic Behaviour," *Oxford Economic Papers*, 1939, reprinted in *Oxford Studies in the Price Mechanism*, ed. T. Wilson and P. W. S. Andrews (Oxford, 1951); P. M. Sweezy, "Demand under Conditions of Oligopoly," *Journal of Political Economy*, 1939, reprinted in *Readings in Price Theory*, ed. G. J. Stigler and K. E. Boulding (London, 1953).

Note that Joan Robinson had already considered the kinked demand curve as an abstract case, in *The Economics of Imperfect Competition* (London, 1933), p. 38.

the existing price. This demand curve seems to him very elastic with respect to a price increase, because he is afraid that, if he raised his price, his immediate rivals would try to deprive him of some of his customers by not following suit. Conversely, the demand curve seems to our businessman to be rigid with respect to a price reduction, because he feels that, if he were to lower his price, his rivals would at once do the same so as not to lose their own customers. Consequently, marginal revenue is discontinuous below the kink in the demand curve. The price is not determined on the basis of equality between marginal revenue and cost, but according to what Hall and Hitch call the full-cost principle and Andrews, following up their work, calls the normal-cost principle.[7]

Hall and Hitch summarize pricing as follows: "Prime (or 'direct') cost per unit is taken as the base, a percentage addition is made to cover overheads (or 'oncost,' or 'indirect' cost), and a further conventional addition (frequently 10 per cent.) is made for profit." [8]

Our argument will benefit if we at once translate this procedure into a formula. Let x be the quantity produced, v the average direct cost (prime or variable cost per unit), q' the percentage of markup destined to cover fixed cost k, and q'' the markup going to net profit g.[9]

The price p is then

$$p = v + q'v + q''v,$$

where

$$q'v = k/x$$

and

$$q''v = g.$$

Let

$$q = (q' + q'');$$

then

$$p = v + qv,$$

where

$$qv = k/x + g.$$

[7] P. W. S. Andrews, *Manufacturing Business* (London, 1949), chap. 5, pgh. 3.
[8] "Price Theory," p. 113.
[9] Direct cost consists of the cost of labor, raw materials, and power. Fixed cost is depreciation charges plus administrative expenses (including managerial salaries).

In reality the volume of output is not constant over time. From the very moment that the entrepreneur acquires his plant, he knows full well that his sales, at constant prices, will fluctuate seasonally and cyclically. What quantity does he consider when he fixes his price? The question is fundamental, because fixed cost, while fixed *globally*, varies per unit with variations in x.

The quantity which the businessman considers is smaller than the maximum possible output (x_m) of his plant and certainly larger than that volume of output (x_0) which would just cover total (overhead plus direct) cost,[10] thus implying zero net profit:

$$p = v + k/x_0;$$

$$x_0 = \frac{k}{p - v}.$$

Therefore, the quantity underlying the price calculation with a view to a net profit, which is what the businessman expects to sell "on the average" or "normally" and which we shall call x_n, lies between x_m and x_0:

$$x_m > x_n > x_0.$$

Accordingly, $qv > k/x_n$ or, more precisely,

$$qv = k/x_n + g.$$

(We shall have occasion to return to these formulas later.)

Hall and Hitch say that in fixing the price, and especially in determining the percentage of addition for profits (q''), each entrepreneur thinks of his potential competitors.[11] Once the price is fixed, it remains on that level by tacit agreement.[12] Not one of the businessmen is inclined to change the price for fear of the reactions of his existing rivals, except when there are cost changes which affect all firms, "such as a change in wages or the price of materials, or if a new process is generally adopted." [13] Hall and Hitch, and also Sweezy, use the hypothesis of a kinked demand curve for their formal explanation of the reason why busi-

[10] The x_0 corresponds to the breakeven point of English and American cost accounting.
[11] "Price Theory," p. 123.
[12] *Ibid.*, p. 113.
[13] *Ibid.*, p. 121.

nessmen are unwilling to alter a price once it is established in the manner described above. Hall and Hitch believe that the situation they describe is very frequent in the market for manufactures. It is a situation of "imperfect competition with oligopoly," as they call it, and in substance corresponds to what we have called differentiated oligopoly.

Competition is imperfect insofar as each businessman can always count on some of his custom: if he raises the price he will not lose all his customers, and if he lowers it he can attract only some of the customers of others. This is expressed by the kinked demand curve. There is oligopoly insofar as each businessman's behavior is ruled mainly by his preoccupation with the reactions of his rivals. However, this preoccupation is not spelled out in complicated conjectures, but comes down to the simple slogan, "Let sleeping dogs lie."

The Hall-Hitch solution does not contradict the solution of marginal analysis. Once it is assumed that at the existing price marginal revenue is discontinuous, it is simply not possible for the individual oligopolist to fix the price on the basis of equality between marginal revenue and marginal cost. The price is determined in another manner and remains at its set level for the whole interval in which marginal cost is lower than marginal revenue in comparison with hypothetical higher prices, and higher than marginal revenue in comparison with hypothetical lower prices.

However, while the Hall-Hitch solution does not contradict the solution of marginal analysis, it is different. The kinked demand curve and the discontinuity of marginal revenue provide a rational justification of the supposed constancy of a price which, in practice, is determined according to the full-cost (or normal-cost) principle and not according to considerations deriving from marginal analysis:

many, perhaps most [of the entrepreneurs questioned] apparently make no effort, even implicitly, to estimate elasticities of demand or marginal (as opposed to average prime) cost; and of those who do, the majority considered the information of little or no relevance to the pricing process, save perhaps in very exceptional conditions.[14]

[14] *Ibid.*, p. 112.

More than once in the past, economists and statisticians have had their doubts whether marginal analysis, although unexceptionable from the point of view of strict logic, was satisfactory from the point of view of realism, at least with reference to the problem of the equilibrium of the firm. But this was the first time that this doubt was corroborated by a broad empirical investigation conducted over the course of several years and with the participation of a group of first-rate economists fully conversant with pure theory.[15] Subsequent empirical research confirmed that businessmen do in fact adopt the full-cost principle.[16] A controversy started over the marginal principle which still continues.

Some economists, such as Machlup, entered the lists as staunch defenders of traditional marginal analysis; others, such as Lester, went so far as to deny it all usefulness, which is a patent and unacceptable exaggeration; still others tried, as indeed Hall and Hitch had done in general terms, to reconcile marginal analysis with the full-cost principle. This principle has already gone far in economics. We need only recall that those who accepted it include Chamberlin[17] and Joan Robinson,[18] who between them have contributed more than any other modern economists to the refinement of the tools of marginal analysis and have applied them to the study of market forms other than competition. They are among those who do not think that the full-cost principle contradicts marginal analysis, but they have not so far constructed a viable bridge between the two.[19]

[15] Hall and Hitch introduce their paper by declaring that they are presenting and building upon facts collected and discussed by the group.
See R. F. Harrod's detailed account of the investigation, in which he took part, in *Economic Essays* (London, 1952), introduction.
[16] See, for example, *Cost Behavior and Price Policy*, National Bureau of Economic Research (New York, 1943), pp. 277–9.
[17] E. H. Chamberlin, "Full Cost and Monopolistic Competition," *Economic Journal*, June 1952.
[18] Joan Robinson, *The Accumulation of Capital* (London, 1956), chap. 19. I would like to thank Mrs. Robinson for allowing me to read this work in proof, and I avail myself of this opportunity to acknowledge a debt to her which far exceeds anything suggested by specific quotations here.
[19] Various other attempts have been made to construct such a bridge or, more generally, to define the rational basis of the full-cost principle: Harrod, *Economic Essays;* S. Lombardini, *Il monopolio nella teoria economica* (Milan, 1953), pp. 234–8; A. Henderson, "The Theory of Duopoly," *Quarterly Journal of Economics*, November 1954; J. P. De Bodt, *La formation des prix:*

The Hall-Hitch solution seems to err on the opposite side from the marginal solution. It is more realistic, but its logic leaves something to be desired. In particular, the theory of the kinked demand curve, while telling us that the price, once fixed at a level acceptable to all entrepreneurs, tends to stay where it is (and changes only when some cost element changes for all of them), does not tell us *why* the price is what it is. Nor does the full-cost principle accomplish this because, owing to different techniques, costs are not equal in all firms and because it assumes, without explaining, the amount of the two markups to be added to variable cost for the purpose of covering fixed cost and earning a profit. Hall and Hitch expressly admit this, but they do not go beyond the merest indication of the reasons for the indeterminacy of these margins.[20] They simply assert, in general terms, that the price will be maintained at the level corresponding to full cost and will not be raised for fear of existing or potential rivals. Thus they conclude: "We cannot say precisely what this price will be, for reasons already explained; if it is set anywhere over a fairly wide range it will have a tendency to stay there." [21]

Much the same may be said of Paul Sweezy, who propounds and elaborates only the hypothesis of the kinked demand curve:

[In this article] no attempt is made to explain how the current price and output situation came about except as it may be explained by reference to a previously existing situation. This is unavoidable since imagined demand curves, unlike the ordinary demand curves of economic analysis, can only be thought of with reference to a given starting-point.[22]

Sweezy adds that, unless price and quantity are given, the problem is undetermined or, more precisely, overdetermined:

Generally speaking, there may be any number of price-output combinations which constitute equilibriums in the sense that, *ceteris paribus*, there is no tendency for the oligopolist to move away from them. But which of these combinations will be actually established in practice, depends upon the previous history of the case.[23]

Analyse des rapports entre la théorie et la politique industrielle (Brussels, 1956).

[20] "Price Theory," p. 114.

[21] *Ibid.*, p. 120.

[22] "Demand under Conditions of Oligopoly," pp. 408–9.

[23] *Ibid.*, p. 409.

This may well be true and in any case requires thought. But the question is whether theory cannot say something more about the "previously existing situation" and about the "previous history."

Direct cost and marginal cost

Let us look at the elements of the formula which express the full-cost or normal-cost principle. The simplest element which serves as a basis for price determination is direct or variable cost. Average direct cost can and must be sharply distinguished from marginal direct cost — which is generally and more briefly just called marginal cost — only when the latter is not constant. When average direct cost is constant, it coincides with marginal direct cost. In that case the first adjective — average or marginal — becomes redundant.

Recent empirical research in the United States has shown that marginal cost is constant, at least over the broad interval which is relevant for the producer, in the majority of manufacturing industries.[24] In other words, the firms making up these industries generally operate in conditions of decreasing average total cost, even in the neighborhood of capacity output. Nowadays many economists accept this conclusion and in their theoretical analyses often use the assumption of constant marginal (or average direct) cost.[25]

[24] See *Cost Behavior and Price Policy,* chap. 5; H. Staehle, "The Measurement of Statistical Cost Functions: An Appraisal of Some Recent Contributions," *American Economic Review,* 1942, reprinted in *Readings in Price Theory,* p. 273; R. B. Heflebower, "Full Costs, Cost Changes, and Prices," *Business Concentration and Price Policy,* p. 370f.

[25] One does not need the results of empirical investigations to understand that in the majority of industries (other than mining), as well as in trade, marginal cost is constant. It is quite enough to peruse any work on cost accounting, where total cost is graphically represented by an ascending straight line, which means that marginal cost is taken as constant (for example, C. B. Nickerson, *Cost Accounting,* New York, 1954, p. 276f; W. B. Lawrence, *Cost Accounting,* New York, 1954, chap. 22). Now these works are written by professionals, with a long experience of business administration, who cannot generally be accused of ignorance of economic theory; they often discuss the theoreticians' assumption that marginal cost is not constant and therefore has to be distinguished from direct cost, and discard it for convincing reasons (see, for example, the remarks by Willers, which are quoted in part in note 27).

If anyone should be tempted to put these works aside because he thinks

Businessmen, then, do not deserve the accusation that they take no account of marginal cost;[26] they do take account of it when they consider direct cost, since this *is* marginal cost.

The traditional thesis, according to which marginal cost must necessarily rise from a certain point on, rests on an extension of the principle of diminishing returns, the fixed factor (in the short period) being plant and equipment. The following arguments are usually adduced in support of this thesis: (1) a growing number of workers operating with given equipment yields decreasing returns after a certain point; (2) overtime work, such as night shifts, commands higher wages; (3) most firms have some rather antiquated machinery which they use only in periods of extraordinary activity; (4) if production is expanded beyond a certain point, plant and equipment become subject to exceptional wear and tear, and user cost rises.

The first argument can be rejected out of hand. The principle of diminishing returns, which was first proposed for agriculture, cannot be extended to the industrial firm, where, in the short period, plant and equipment are supposed to be the constant factor. Barring quite exceptional cases, the number of workers per machine is fixed. A machine cannot be compared with land, where, within certain limits, labor can be added or withdrawn at will. The second and third arguments are true, but the situations they envisage imply not continuously rising marginal cost, *but marginal cost rising stepwise, remaining constant on each tread*. Moreover, these situations are proper to unusually intense ac-

---

they sin on the side of empiricism, let him remember two things: (1) to lay claim to being scientific, a proposition needs not only formal validity but also a certain degree of realism, and these works show quite clearly that the assumption of varying marginal cost normally does not correspond to reality; (2) Marshall, who was a theoretician of great stature, did not disdain the study of works on business accounting, and when he constructed his concept of prime cost he took it precisely from such a work (Garcke and Fells, *Factory Accounts,* chap. 1; see Marshall, *Principles of Economics,* Book V, chap. 4, pgh. 5).

In works on cost accounting it is usual to distinguish three categories of cost: fixed cost, variable or direct cost, and semivariable cost. The third category has no particular relevance to our argument, and we shall therefore exclude it.

[26] This charge has been leveled, too, at writers on business administration. See, for example, C. Bresciani-Turroni, *Corso di economia politica* (2nd ed., Milan, 1954), I, 271.

tivity, such as at the height of a boom, and therefore cannot be
taken as a reference base in considering the problem of equilibrium.[27] For the same reason, the fourth argument is also unacceptable. Furthermore, it would seem that in practice businessmen and accountants regard the methodical calculation of changes
in user cost not only as problematic but as unjustifiably costly,
even in periods of intense activity; as a rule, they prefer to include this item in depreciation.[28]

The fact that marginal (or direct) cost is constant for the
interval relevant to the entrepreneur and in normal conditions
(of equilibrium) is further proof that in modern industrial situations competition is a limiting case which, as we know, occurs but
rarely. Constant marginal cost, according to traditional marginal
analysis, is incompatible with the conditions of perfect competition.

Marginal cost, in this context, refers to the short period, when
plant and machinery are assumed to be given. Contrary to traditional theory, which assumes the short-run marginal-cost curve
to be U-shaped, there are, as we have seen, good reasons to believe that it is constant, at least in the interval relevant for the
entrepreneur.[29]

[27] It is worth while to quote here a passage from a recent work on business
administration, R. Willers, *The Dynamics of Industrial Management* (New
York, 1954), p. 317: "The remark has sometimes been made that, as production increases, productivity decreases and that therefore the trend of a
(total) variable expense in relation to sales should not be a straight line but an
upward skewed curve.

"The experience of industrial life does not seem to confirm this view. If a
plant was operated in such a way as to become crowded, which as a rule is a
sign of poor management, such a condition might conceivably develop, but it
would then be one of these exceptional cases for which the normal procedures
of management and control do not apply.

"On the basis of repeated experience, it can be said that for all practical
purposes, the trend of a (total) variable expense in relation to production can
be considered as represented by a straight line within the limits within which
a plan *actually* operates."

[28] See Robinson, *Accumulation of Capital*, chap. 19. Also, *Report . . . of the
Subcommittee on Antitrust and Monopoly*, 85th Congress, 2nd Session, November 1, 1958, "Administered Prices — Automobiles," p. 116: "In general, maintenance and repair expenses will vary somewhat with the degree of utilization
of capacity, but never is there a directly proportional relationship."

[29] In traditional theory, the total cost function is of the type,

$$C = ax^3 - bx^2 + cx + k,$$

According to traditional theory, the marginal-cost curve is also U-shaped in the long period, when marginal cost includes the fixed costs of the short period and determines the long-run supply curve. Up to a certain point, marginal cost decreases as a result of economies of scale; thereafter it increases because of the growing difficulties of organization and administration in a steadily expanding firm (the diseconomies of scale). There can be no doubt that, at least up to a point, technically conditioned economies of scale do operate; on the other hand, it is far less certain that organizational and administrative difficulties necessarily cause the curve to rise again. One can think of many organizational devices which have in fact been applied to remedy these difficulties or, at any rate, to prevent them from growing more than proportionately with the size of the firm. What is true is that, at any given stage of technology, there is an objective limit to the size of plant: at some point no bigger plant can be designed and built, for the simple reason that the technicians do not know how to do it. If a firm wants to produce more than is technologically possible for its biggest plant to put out, two or three such plants must be taken into service, which means that beyond this limit long-run marginal cost becomes constant. However, beyond that limit we can no longer speak of a marginal-cost curve, but only of a series of discrete points. Indeed, if the series of smaller plants corresponding to different technologies is not continuous — that is, if there is no gradual transition from one plant to the next — then we cannot properly speak of a curve even on this side of the limit represented by the biggest plant. In these conditions there is, in strict analysis, no such thing as a long-run supply curve. We shall have occasion to return to this later.

---

which implies that average total cost, marginal cost, and average direct cost all have U-shaped functions, though each is different from the others. According to the argument in the text, the total cost function can, in first approximation, be assumed to be of the type,

$$C = vx + k,$$

which implies decreasing average total cost up to the capacity limit of plant and constant, as well as equal, marginal, and direct, cost.

Comparison between the full-cost formula and the formula of marginal analysis

If marginal cost, m, coincides with direct cost, our previous formula,

$$p = v + qv, \tag{1.1}$$

becomes

$$p = m + qm,$$

or

$$q = \frac{p - m}{m}. \tag{1.2}$$

This equation can easily be translated into the familiar formula according to which, under monopolistic conditions, marginal revenue and marginal cost are equal:

$$p - \frac{p}{\eta} = m. \tag{1.3}$$

Hence, the "degree of monopoly" has been defined as the inverse of the elasticity of demand:

$$\frac{1}{\eta} = \frac{p - m}{p}. \tag{1.4}$$

If we divide (2) by (4) we get:

$$q\eta = \frac{p}{m},$$

or

$$q = \frac{p}{\eta m}. \tag{1.5}$$

We see that q and η depend on the same variables, p and m; in equilibrium, and provided we know p and m, q can immediately be translated into η and vice versa. Does, then, the business-man's formula (1.1) coincide with that (1.3) of the theoretician of marginal analysis? Is it a fallacy to oppose actual business procedure and the results of marginal analysis? Is the long and involved and still very lively debate on the marginal analysis founded only on a misunderstanding?

We shall see that in fact some economists have worked out an analysis where the businessman's q and the theoretician's η are interchangeable. This may appear plausible at first sight, insofar as in every market certain forces enter into the determination of q which, in a sense, might be summed up in the concept of degree of monopoly. But, as we shall see later, q and η can be resolved into each other only at the cost of a complete perversion of the meaning of demand curve and elasticity of demand, which are and can be founded only on the tastes of consumers. Moreover, the essence of the problem of oligopoly is the question of how q is determined and what its limits are. To assume *a priori* that q can be translated into terms of elasticity of demand means to take as given precisely what is to be solved.

Andrews' treatment of q, which he calls the costing margin, is unsatisfactory. He does not really go beyond the assertion, already made by Hall and Hitch (see Chapter 1), that this margin is "determined by competition" and by competition not only from existing but also from potential rivals.[30] It goes without saying that Andrews means by competition something very different from the "perfect" or "pure" competition of the marginalists.

Harrod, in his turn, constructed a model in which he ingeniously tried to reconcile marginal theory with the results of empirical research, and to do so not in the general and formal manner of Hall and Hitch, but systematically.[31] Harrod's analysis is elegant, but it cannot be said to have solved the problem of the level of q and hence of the price. Like Hall and Hitch and like Andrews, Harrod assumes without rigorous proof that if the entrepreneur "raises the price appreciably above direct cost plus overhead cost he will render his market vulnerable." "It is true that he might for a brief interval enjoy a rather higher rate of profit"; but in the long period the market will be invaded by new producers and the entrepreneur's profit will be less, not more, than before. This, he states, amounts to saying that the "long-period demand curve is flatter than the short-period demand curve."

Bain, who has contributed the most significant writing on the

[30] Andrews, *Manufacturing Business*, p. 153f.
[31] Harrod, *Economic Essays*, p. 161f.

problem of oligopoly,[32] rightly emphasizes the importance of studying the conditions of entry. Indeed, as long as we assume a fixed and unalterable number of firms, we are led either to place disproportionate stress on the demand curve and on demand elasticity or to go back to the psychological-reaction curves. It would seem a more fruitful approach to an adequate explanation of the equilibrium price, and thus of the level of the markup q, to drop that assumption. Our analysis of price determination, like Bain's, will concentrate on the conditions of entry.

[32] Before his book *Barriers to New Competition* (discussed in my preface), Joe S. Bain published several articles on our problem, including, "A Note on Pricing in Monopoly and Oligopoly" (*American Economic Review,* March 1949), "Conditions of Entry and the Emergence of Monopoly" (in *Monopoly, Competition, and Their Regulation,* ed. E. H. Chamberlin for the International Economic Association, London, 1954), and "Economies of Scale, Concentration, and the Condition of Entry in Twenty Manufacturing Industries" (*American Economic Review,* March 1954).

II

Price Determination

In the hypothesis of a kinked demand curve, the price and the output of each oligopolistic firm are data. It follows that the structure of the industry — that is, the distribution of output among the various firms — is also known. But how do that price and that structure come about? This is the problem to be solved. It is a long-term problem, insofar as we must allow not only for changes in any existing firm's plant and machinery but also for the entry of new firms and, hence, for changes in the structure of the industry. Once this question is resolved and we have thereby explained how each firm determines q, then q becomes a datum for the short period and, as such, provides guidance to each firm on how to modify its price when direct cost changes.

Outline of the proposed solution

In trying to work out our solution, we shall begin with the long-term problem, the fundamental one. We shall discuss it in the setting of a highly concentrated industry, with one or a few large firms and several or many medium and small firms — that is, in a situation of relatively concentrated oligopoly.

For the sake of simplicity, we consider a single product and, initially, completely neglect product differentiation and, hence, consumer preferences for certain firms. We distinguish between demand and elasticity of demand with respect to the industry and with respect to individual oligopolistic firms.[1] (If we neglect product differentiation, there is no demand curve for the individual firm as distinct from the demand curve for the industry.)

[1] See Chamberlin, *The Theory of Monopolistic Competition,* p. 90 f; M. A. Copeland, "The Theory of Monopolistic Competition," *Journal of Political Economy,* no. 4 (1934), p. 531.

Only the industry demand curve can be said to reflect the tastes and thus the possible reactions of consumers. The individual demand curve reflects a mixture of consumer reactions and of reactions of the firm's (existing and potential) competitors. It is a spurious or, as Kaldor and Sweezy say, an "imagined" demand curve.

We consider the long-period demand curve for the industry. Anybody proposing to enter the market must reckon not only with the present size of demand, but must also make some estimate of the market's capacity to absorb an additional quantity of goods — either (a) at lower prices if the market is stationary, (b) at the ruling price if the market tends to expand, or (c) at lower prices if the market tends to expand but the entrant wants to speed up its expansion. Formally, in case (a) the problem is that of the shape of a given demand curve and of movements along it; in case (b) the problem is that of shifts of the demand curve, in relation to growing consumer incomes; case (c) is a combination of the other two problems. In case (a) the analytical tool to be used is the price elasticity of demand, in case (b) the income elasticity of demand. For the purposes of price determination, we shall consider only case (a).

Finally, we shall try to identify such objective elements as may, in real situations, serve as a basis for price determination. Otherwise, we would run the danger of remaining in the fantastic world of reaction curves and conjectural variations — a world where everything might and nothing need happen. And we would risk propounding explanations which may be formally correct but of little or no help in a concrete analysis of any particular industry. The only result would be a perpetuation of the serious gap between the theoretical models of oligopoly and modern industrial realities. Without an objective base our explanation, like others before it, would not escape from the vicious circle and would be wide open to R. A. Gordon's sharp rebuke:

Refuge in subjective interpretations of the cost and revenue functions is certainly no answer. It leaves theory saying that businessmen do what they do because they do it.[2]

[2] "Short-period Price Determination," *American Economic Review,* June 1948, p. 287.

We shall seek to show that the fundamental objective element of price determination in the case of concentrated oligopoly is technology.

Technological discontinuities

In the theory of oligopoly, as in most theoretical analysis, it is generally explicitly or implicitly assumed that factors of production are continuously substitutable. The assumption admittedly does not correspond to reality, but it is at least thought not to involve errors which prejudice the results of the analysis. Accordingly, indifference curves for producers — isoquants — have been introduced alongside the indifference curves for consumers. Let us see whether this assumption is admissible in the treatment of the oligopoly problem.

We may with advantage remind ourselves of the warning uttered by Vilfredo Pareto, who contributed more than any other economist to the propagation of the use of indifference curves:

Problems involving infinitesimal quantity variations are much easier to deal with than problems concerning finite quantity variations. *Whenever it can be done,* the former should be substituted for the latter.[3]

Can it be done in the case of oligopoly, and especially in the case of oligopoly resulting from the process of industrial concentration? The answer is that it cannot be done as a matter of principle. The characteristic feature of the process of industrial concentration is precisely that it creates by no means negligible technological discontinuities. Only large firms can apply certain methods, both technical and organizational, and only large firms can realize certain economies of scale. And the transition from small to large firms is not gradual; there are jumps and the jumps become broader as concentration proceeds.

Many economists now consider these technological discontinuities important enough to warrant special analytical tools, whereby these discontinuities can be introduced into economic theory and their consequences explained. One example of this development is linear programming. The assumption of discontinuity in factor proportions underlies some recent models pur-

[3] *Manuale di economia politica* (Milan, 1906), p. 169. (My italics.)

porting to explain structural unemployment in underdeveloped economies.[4]

However, the assumption of discontinuities has not been developed much in the theory of market forms or, more especially, in the theory of oligopoly. Many economists mention it, but to my knowledge only three scholars have treated it with the attention it deserves: two economists, Alberto Breglia[5] and Nicholas Kaldor,[6] and one economic historian, Hermann Levy.[7] The kind of discontinuity which is relevant to our problem has been concisely described by Paul Rosenstein-Rodan in a recent paper:

> Probably, the assumption of rigidly fixed coefficients is realistic only for some industries. Similarly, continuous variability of the coefficients is certainly an exceptional case. The most realistic assumption for the greater part of industry seems to be that of limited and discontinuous variability of coefficients. We assume, therefore, that for a large number of industries factors of production can be combined in three alternative proportions, defining three different points on the isoquant curve:
>   a) High capital intensity (example: automatic looms), corresponding to very high productivity of labor;
>   b) "normal" capital intensity (example: ordinary looms), corresponding, generally, to high productivity of labor;
>   c) very low capital intensity (example: hand looms), corresponding to very low productivity of labor.[8]

Criteria and assumptions of the model

To deal with the problem of the equilibrium price over a long period and in conditions of oligopoly, we shall proceed rather like Walras with his *prix crié par hasard*. We shall start out from a given structure of industry and from a given price, and ask ourselves whether that structure and that price are in equilibrium and can remain unchanged. If not, we shall look for the equilibrium. By "structure" of an industry we mean: (a) the

---

[4] R. S. Eckaus, "The Factor Proportions Problem in Underdeveloped Areas," *American Economic Review*, September 1955.

[5] "Cenni di teoria della politica economica," *Giornale degli economisti*, 1934, reprinted in *Temi di economia e vita sociale* (Milan, 1942), pp. 349–52.

[6] "Market Imperfection and Excess Capacity," pp. 42–3.

[7] *Monopoly and Competition*, pp. 299–302; *The New Industrial System*, pp. 156–8.

[8] "Rapporti fra fattori produttivi nell'economia italiana," *L'industria*, no. 4 (1954), pp. 463–70.

absolute size of the market, that is, the volume of sales at a given price; (b) the absorption capacity of the market in the narrow sense previously specified (price elasticity of demand); (c) the distribution of sales among a number of firms of different types.

Concerning the first point, we shall see that the absolute size of the market conditions the equilibrium structure of the industry. This aspect has wrongly been neglected in the theoretical analysis of oligopoly. Concerning the second point, we shall use a special concept of elasticity, which we call "empirical elasticity" and which, unlike infinitesimal but like finite elasticity, allows for discrete changes in price and quantity. As will be seen from the model we shall try to construct, the consideration of discrete changes becomes necessary in the hypothesis of technological discontinuities.

The formula of infinitesimal elasticity is well known:

$$\eta = -\frac{p}{x} \Big/ \frac{dp}{dx}.$$

Various notions of finite elasticity are conceivable. One of them is the ratio between the percentage variations of quantity and price. Another is arc elasticity of demand.[9] The formulas for finite elasticity have the advantage of greater realism, precisely because they concern finite variations. But for us, at any rate, they have the disadvantage of dealing only with price and quantity variations and neglecting the size and changes of total revenue. Yet when a businessman wants to estimate the possible or probable consequences of some (not infinitesimal) change in price or quantity, the thing of immediate interest to him is to compare the total revenue he can expect from the two pairs of prices and output. The simplest way to express the comparison is the ratio of the two amounts of total revenue. We have to choose the proper numerator and denominator of this ratio.

We know that when infinitesimal elasticity equals unity, total revenue does not vary with changes in price (or quantity); when infinitesimal elasticity is less than unity, total revenue rises when

[9] See R. G. D. Allen, "The Concept of Arc Elasticity of Demand," *Review of Economic Studies,* June 1934, pp. 226–9.

price rises and falls when price falls, and vice versa when infinitesimal elasticity exceeds unity. To get analogous results, we must take as numerator in our ratio the total revenue expressed by the product of lower price (p_1) times larger output (x_2), and as the denominator the total revenue expressed by the product of higher price (p_2) times lower output (x_1). Thus the "empirical elasticity of demand," e, is:

$$e = \frac{p_1 x_2}{p_2 x_1}.$$

This is the concept of elasticity which we shall use throughout. It is entirely different from the traditional concept of elasticity; the only common feature is the behavior of total revenue, according to whether elasticity — in our or in the traditional concept — equals unity or is lower or higher than unity.

Concerning the third point (the existence of firms of different types), we adopt a subdivision of technologies similar to Rosenstein-Rodan's and suppose that every group of firms uses only one organizational method and only one kind of fixed capital.

We assume that new firms may enter the market and existing ones may expand; but, so as not to complicate the model too much, we assume that if a firm expands it does so by setting up new establishments exactly equal to those already in operation.[10] Thus, every group of firms represents one type of technology. To each type of technology there corresponds an establishment of given size, capable of producing a volume of output not exceeding a certain upper limit: output can vary, but not beyond the technological limit.

In making the assumption of a given number of technologies, we preclude innovations: any new firm is obliged to adopt one of the existing technologies, and its output will have the corresponding upper limit. Direct cost is taken as constant up to that limit and so equals marginal cost.

We assume that total and average fixed cost are higher and average direct cost lower in proportion as the maximum output which each firm can produce is larger. The largest firms are the

[10] This means that we assume that the so-called law of harmony is operative. Erich Schneider, *Theorie der Produktion* (Vienna, 1934), p. 51f.

most efficient, in the sense that their average total cost is lower, their higher average fixed cost being more than compensated for by their lower direct cost.[11] We shall consider, then, a situation of concentrated oligopoly and, more precisely, oligopoly with *relative* concentration; the case of oligopoly with *absolute* concentration is simpler and can be analyzed on the same lines as the more complex case.

Firms of different size have unequal power to influence prices. We might assume that only the large firms can fix the price and that the others do no more than adapt their supply, so that price remains stable. This is what is meant by price leadership.[12] But it seems more realistic to assume instead that, while smaller firms are unable to fix the price directly, they can influence it indirectly by variations in their aggregate output. If the firms are very small, none of them can cause any appreciable price change and the situation in this respect is like competition; but if the number of small firms changes, the price will vary considerably, notwithstanding the fact that the supply of each single small firm is minute.

We therefore assume that only the large firms can directly fix the price and that other firms influence it indirectly through variations in their aggregate output. This means that, unless the price fixed by the large firms is an equilibrium price, it will not last. In the face of the action of small firms, only an equilibrium price can last. Nevertheless, as our subsequent analysis will show, the power of the large firms to fix the price directly has very significant consequences: it affects the very conditions of equilibrium in the oligopolistic market.

Finally, we assume that new firms are induced to enter the market (and existing firms to stay in it) only if in the long run they anticipate and gradually actually achieve a profit rate at least equal to a certain minimum.

[11] Strictly speaking, the assumption of a finite number of technologies — each of which is adopted by a given group of firms — rules out the possibility of drawing a long-run supply *curve*. Instead, we have a finite series of points corresponding to minimum total average cost for each type of technology (see above, p. 29).

[12] See Bresciani-Turroni, *Corso di economia politica,* II, part V, chap. 2.

Rate of profit, entry-preventing price, and elimination price

Let us consider the rate of profit over cost:

$$r = \frac{px - k - vx}{k + vx},\qquad(2.1)$$

where px is total revenue, k total fixed cost, and vx total variable cost, all expressed in annual terms.

If the minimum profit rate is r_m and we know the fixed cost, variable cost, and output of a given firm, the price corresponding to the minimum profit rate for that firm is:

$$p_m x = r_m k + r_m vx + k,$$

or

$$p_m = \left(\frac{k}{x} + v\right)(1 + r_m).\qquad(2.2)$$

If the price leaders intend to prevent the entry of new firms of a given type, they must keep the price below the level which would give the new firms their minimum profit rate: the "entry-preventing price," p_c, is lower than p_m.

If the price leaders intend to squeeze out existing firms, they must fix the price at a level below the variable cost of the firms they want to eliminate: a firm can survive for some time if the price is so low that fixed cost cannot be recouped, but it can remain in the market for only a relatively short period if the price falls below variable cost, requiring disbursements at short intervals. The "elimination price" is lower than the variable cost of the firms to be eliminated ($p_e < v$). Strictly speaking, this is the short-run elimination price. In the long run, any price lower than p_m for any given type of firm will cause the firm gradually to abandon the market. In other words, the long-run elimination price coincides with the entry-preventing price.

We shall see later in what conditions the price leaders have an interest in wanting to coexist with other firms and in what conditions it is better for them to engage in an elimination war. In order to avoid unnecessary complications, however, we shall suppose that in the latter case the price leaders consider the short-run rather than the long-run elimination price (which they will use only as an entry-preventing price). Only when examining the consequences of quantity variations, which affect prices indirectly, do we allow for the possibility that, in the long period, certain firms are in fact eliminated when the price falls below p_m.

Long-run equilibrium in concentrated oligopoly

We are now in a position to define the conditions of long-run equilibrium in a situation of oligopoly characterized by a high degree of concentration of firms. The problem is complicated not only because we have introduced so many assumptions, but because we must consider alternative adaptation reactions. For this reason mathematical treatment appears rather difficult (at least to me) and, because it would compel us to adopt greatly simplified assumptions, the result might not repay the effort. Numerical treatment would seem to entail no sacrifice in rigor and may have the advantage of greater simplicity and clarity.

Let us assume that the structure of industry, *crié par hasard,* is as follows:

Number and size of firms	Output of each firm	Output of the group
20 small	100	2,000
2 medium	1,000	2,000
1 large	8,000	8,000
		12,000 ("market size")

Let the initial price be 20 and the elasticity of demand equal unity (the value of total sales does not change when price changes). Let there be three types of technology and hence three types of firms, in ascending order of intensity of fixed capital; for each type of firms the costs, which depend on the technology, and the profits (per unit of output and as a percentage of total cost) are shown in the table below. The maximum output of which each type of firm is capable is shown in column 1. Note that while there is a maximum output, there is, from the technological point of view, no minimum output. Actual output is, in each case, determined by the entrepreneur's profit, and it *may* be less than maximum output. This implies that the existence of unutilized capacity is compatible with equilibrium. The greater is the gap between maximum and actual output, that is, the less the degree of utilization of plant, the higher is the average fixed

Costs and profits of three types of firm

Out-put x	Fixed cost Total k	Aver-age k/x	Aver-age direct cost v	Total cost $T=k+vx$	Price p	Total revenue px	Total $G=px-T$	Per unit g	Profit rate (%) $s=G/T$
100	100	1	17.5	1,850	20	2,000	150	1.5	8.1
					19.5	1,950	100	1	5.4
					19.4	1,940	90	0.9	5.0
1,000	2,000	2	16	18,000	20	20,000	2,000	2	11.1
					19.5	19,500	1,500	1.5	8.3
					19.4	19,400	1,400	1.4	7.8
					19.2	19,200	1,200	1.2	6.7
8,000	24,000	3	14	136,000	20	160,000	24,000	3	17.6
					19.5	156,000	20,000	2.5	14.7
					19.4	155,200	19,200	2.4	14.1
					19.2	153,600	17,600	2.2	12.9
6,385	24,000	3.76	14	113,400	18.8	120,040	6,640	1.04	5.8

cost k/x, because any reduction in x causes k/x to rise and unit profit to fall; but the entrepreneur may find it profitable to produce less than maximum output if, at a given price and sales volume, he can get a higher total profit than he could get by producing and selling his maximum output. In this sense a volume of output falling short of maximum output can be equilibrium output. The minimum profit rate is 5 percent.[13]

[13] The concept of a minimum profit rate has its bearing on the controversial question of profit maximization. Some economists, including Hall and Hitch, deny that entrepreneurs aim at maximizing profit as defined by marginal analysis and say that entrepreneurs are swayed by other considerations. However, if we look more closely at these other considerations, all they come down to is that entrepreneurs tend to maximize profit not in the short but in the long period. We shall return to this question later. We note here that it does not seem that proper attention has been paid to an important and well-defined limit to profit maximization, whether in the short or in the long run: this limit is the minimum profit rate. To illustrate the point, let us suppose that a firm acquires all its factors of production with borrowed funds on which it pays 5 percent interest. The firm subsequently has an opportunity either to invest a further 100, which would yield a profit of 6, or a further 200, yielding a profit of 8. The absolute amount of profit is higher in the second case, but the profit rate of 4 percent compares with 6 percent in the first case. The current rate of interest being 5 percent, the entrepreneur can effect only such investments as yield him at least 5 percent and he will therefore not invest 200.

There are no obstacles to the entry of new firms except as implied by the previous assumptions. If new firms enter the market, the existing ones continue to produce as much as before. They do so not only to discourage the entry of new firms, whose additional output in these circumstances necessarily depresses the price and so makes the whole market less profitable, but also because by lowering their output the existing firms would raise their total average cost (since on our assumptions total average cost is decreasing up to the limit of plant capacity).[14] For the sake of simplicity, we have ruled out any reduction of output by existing firms as a result of the entry of new firms; if existing firms decide to produce less than maximum output, they do so not under pressure from new entry, but on the basis of independent economic calculations.

Now let us see whether the situation so described is an equilibrium situation and, if not, whether we can find one.

The prices, p_m, corresponding to the minimum profit rate of 5 percent are, according to equation (2.2):

	p_m
Small firms	19.4
Medium firms	18.9
Large firms	17.8

The entry-preventing price, p_c, with respect to firms in each group lies immediately below the respective p_m. The elimination price, p_c, lies immediately below the variable cost of each firm. Total sales at the various prices, when empirical elasticity of demand equals unity, are:

price	times	units sold	equals	value of sales
20.0		12,000		
19.5		12,300		
19.2		12,500		
18.8		12,770		240,000
13.3		18,000		
12.0		20,000		

[14] See F. Modigliani, "New Developments on the Oligopoly Front," *Journal of Political Economy*, no. 3 (1958), p. 230.

I. *Quantity variations.* (1) No new large firm can enter the market. If it did, total sales would rise to 20,000 units, the price would fall to 12 and would thus be lower than both the price corresponding to the minimum profit rate (17.8) and the variable cost (14) of large firms.

(2) Even the entry of a new medium-sized firm is precluded. Sales would rise to 13,000 units, the price would fall to 18.4, which is less than p_m for medium firms (18.9).

(3) On the other hand, up to three small firms can enter the market. Their entry would cause sales to rise to 12,300 units and the price to fall to 19.5, which exceeds the price corresponding to the minimum profit rate for small firms (19.4). The entry of a fourth small firm would depress the price below 19.4 and is therefore precluded.

Our assumptions do not admit of a restriction of output below the initial volume for the purpose of obtaining a rise in price, in which case more small firms could enter, or even medium and large ones.

We conclude that our initial 20 is not an equilibrium price. Provisionally, we can regard 19.5 as the equilibrium price.

II. *Price variations.* By assumption, prices can be changed directly only by the large firm.

There is no advantage to be gained from raising the price above the initial level of 20.[15] The large firm would have to restrict its own output, other firms would be attracted, and the whole maneuver would be worse than useless from the point of view of the original firm — it would be positively harmful. (It would be profitable to raise the price only in the presence of obstacles to entry other than those implied by our assumptions: for instance, legal obstacles, such as an outright prohibition for all firms, large or small, to enter the market.) We are led to consider what the large firm may stand to gain by an aggressive price policy, designed to eliminate the small firms or both the medium and small firms, and then to occupy the "economic

---

[15] We have assumed that the elasticity of demand equals unity; but it would not be to the advantage of the large firm to raise the price, *even if demand were very rigid.*

space" so vacated by setting up new establishments exactly equal to the existing large one.

(1) To eliminate the small firms, the large firm must fix the price below their variable cost, at most at 17.4. This price at once lowers the profit of the large firm; the "lost gain" constitutes the cost of the struggle and is all the higher the longer the price must be kept down to 17.4.

The economic space vacated by the small firms corresponds to sales of 2,000 units. This is not enough. With a new large establishment output would rise to 18,000 and the price fall to 13.3, which is less than the large firm's p_m and v. It does not pay the large firm to pursue an aggressive price policy toward the small firms.

(2) If the large firm wants to eliminate all the other firms, medium and small, it must for a certain time keep the price down to 15.9, that is, at a level below the variable cost of medium and, *a fortiori*, small firms. Afterwards, the price can be raised to 18.8, the entry-preventing price for medium and, *a fortiori*, small firms. The cost of the struggle is much higher than in the preceding case. Instead of merely forgoing some of its profit, the large firm sustains an actual loss because, while more than covering variable cost, the price of 15.9 does not cover average total cost.

The disappearance of the small and medium firms leaves a void of 4,000 units. Would it be profitable for the large firm to set up a new establishment, exactly equal to its existing one?

At a price of 18.8, it is possible to sell 12,770 units. If the firm had two establishments, it would have to operate them at less than full capacity. Instead of 8,000, it would have to produce 6,385 per plant. But then average fixed cost would rise from 3 to 3.76. Instead of making a profit of 2.5 (19.5 − 17) on each unit sold, the firm would make only 1.04 (18.8 − 17.76). The total profit for each establishment is 6,640 (1.04 × 6,385), and the total for both establishments together comes to 13,280. This new total profit is less than the firm could previously obtain with a single establishment at a price of 19.5 (20,000).

Hence the large firm has nothing to gain from a price war against all its competitors.

So far, then, we have found only one equilibrium price, 19.5. At this price, the structure of the industry is:

Firms	Output
23 small	2,300
2 medium	2,000
1 large	8,000
	12,300

This result naturally depends on the initial structure and on the assumptions made, which include that of a given absolute size of the market. Little attention is usually paid to the market's absolute size, yet it is one of the elements that determine final equilibrium.

To illustrate this statement, let us consider a situation in which all the previous assumptions hold, except one: the initial size of the market is now assumed to be double the preceding one. In these circumstances the initial structure of the industry is:

Firms	Output
40 small	4,000
4 medium	4,000
2 large	16,000
	24,000

The price at which this quantity is sold is again 20. If elasticity of demand is equal to unity, we have the following price/quantity pairs:

$$\left.\begin{array}{l} 20.0 \times 24,000 \\ 19.4 \times 24,700 \\ 19.3 \times 24,800 \\ 19.2 \times 25,000 \\ 18.8 \times 25,530 \end{array}\right\} \quad 480,000$$

I′. Quantity variations. (1) No new large firms can enter the market, because the price would fall below the entry-preventing level for large firms (17.7).

(2) One new medium-sized firm can enter. The volume of sales rises to 25,000 and the price falls to 19.2, which exceeds the entry-preventing price for medium firms (18.8). However, the price of 19.2 is below the entry-preventing price for small firms (19.3). Thus, not only can no new small firms enter, but in the long

run the existing ones gradually leave the market. The economic space so vacated can be occupied by medium firms up to the number of four. The new structure of the industry will then be:

Firms	Output
0 small	—
4 + 1 + 4 = 9 medium	9,000
2 large	16,000
	25,000

The price can remain at 19.2; it is an equilibrium price.

(3) At the initial price of 20, with the corresponding sales volume of 24,000, seven new small firms can enter. Sales rise to 24,700, and the price falls to a stable level of 19.4. There is not room for more than seven, because in that event the price would fall below the entry-preventing price for small firms. Nor could a new medium firm enter at that point: output would rise to 25,700 and the price fall to 18.7, which is below the entry-preventing price for medium firms.

Hence, if small firms are the first to enter the market, equilibrium output and price are, respectively, 24,700 and 19.4. The structure of the industry will be:

Firms	Output
47 small	4,700
4 medium	4,000
2 large	16,000
	24,700

II'. *Price variations.* As before, the large firms have nothing to gain from price increases. But the large firms may consider the expediency of diminishing the price and thereby eliminating others. We shall assume that the two large firms act in agreement with each other.

(1) If the large firms intend to eliminate the small ones, the price must at first be kept at 17.4 and then, permanently, at a level not higher than 19.3. At that price 24,800 units can be sold, of which 16,000 are produced by the two large firms, 4,000 by the four medium firms still in the market, and the remaining 4,800 by a new establishment set up to this end by the two large firms. But the capacity of each large establishment is 8,000; the two

large firms now have three such establishments between them. If the large firms divide their total sales volume into three equal parts, each plant will produce 6,934 instead of its full-capacity 8,000 (16,000 + 4,800 = 20,800 : 3 = 6,934). At a price of 19.3 each establishment makes a profit of 12,825, and the two firms together obtain a total profit of 12,825 × 3 = 38,475. This profit is higher than the joint profit the two large firms can make with two establishments in the equilibrium situation I' (2) at a price of 19.2 (17,600 × 2 = 35,200), and higher than the joint profit they can make in the equilibrium situation I' (3) at a price of 19.4 (19,200 × 2 = 38,400). But the difference is relatively small and in all likelihood not enough to make good the cost of the struggle (loss of profit during the period when the two large firms must keep the price down to 17.4).

In these circumstances it seems very unlikely that the large firms will have any interest in pursuing an aggressive price policy toward the small firms.

(2) To eliminate all other firms, small and medium, the price must for a certain time be kept at 15.9 (below the variable cost of medium firms). Later the price can be raised to 18.8 (entry-preventing price for medium and, *a fortiori*, small firms). At that price the market absorbs 25,530 units. There is room for three large establishments, one of which will have to be owned jointly by the two firms, as in the preceding case. The three large establishments can produce 24,000; the corresponding price of 20 opens the door to the re-entry of medium-sized and small firms.

(a) There is room for one medium firm only. Output rises to 25,000 and the price falls to 19.2, where it can remain. This equilibrium price is the same as the equilibrium price in case I' (2) above, but the structure of the industry is different:

Firms	Output
0 small	—
1 medium	1,000
2 large (3 establ.)	24,000
	25,000

(b) Alternatively, seven small firms can enter the market.

Output rises to 24,700 and the price falls to 19.4, where it can remain. This is the same equilibrium price as in case I' (3), but again the structure of the industry is different:

Firms	Output
7 small	700
0 medium	—
2 large (3 establ.)	24,000
	24,700

The question remains, now, whether either of the two equilibrium situations reached through the struggle is more or less advantageous to the two large firms than the equilibrium situations I' (2) and I' (3) brought about peacefully and therefore not involving any cost of struggle.

In situation I' (2), with a price of 19.2, each of the two large firms makes a profit of 17,600 and their joint profit is 35,200.

In situation I' (3), with a price of 19.4, each large firm makes a profit of 19,200 and their joint profit is 38,400.

In both the alternative equilibrium situations after the struggle, the joint profit of the two large firms, which now have three instead of two establishments between them (and which, according to our assumption, act in agreement with each other), is not twice but three times the profit which each separate large firm could obtain:

II'(2a) (price 19.2) : 17,600 × 3 = 52,800
II'(2b) (price 19.4) : 19,200 × 3 = 57,600

So the total profit to be expected after a price war is quite markedly higher than the total profit in the absence of a price war. The large firms will launch the struggle if the cost of doing so (which, as we have noted earlier, depends on the length of time for which the price has to be kept below the elimination level) appears less than the capital value of the expected additional profits. This is likely to be so, or at any rate much more likely than in case II' (1).

Hence, all other things being equal, an absolutely larger market leads to different equilibrium situations and increases the likelihood of an aggressive price policy on the part of the large firms, designed to eliminate small and medium firms. Therefore, the larger the market, the larger tends to be the average size of firms and the lower the equilibrium price.

Some comments on the model

We have seen that there are several equilibrium prices. They are equilibrium prices in the sense that once one of them is established, none of the oligopolists has reason to change it. This does not imply that the problem of oligopoly is indeterminate in the commonly accepted use of that term. All it means is that, according to the assumptions made, different — but perfectly determined — equilibrium situations are possible. We may also say that the problem has several solutions; but this statement is not to be understood in the instantaneous (or static) sense. The truth is that the final equilibrium price depends on the assumptions made with regard to the origin of the price and quantity changes. If the changes are initiated by firms of a certain type, the price reaches a certain equilibrium level; if the changes are initiated by other firms, it reaches another equilibrium level. In all cases the initial structure of the industry affects the final equilibrium situation and the variations are irreversible, since they imply, among other things, changes in plant. Once a variation has taken place, it is not possible to go back along the same route. Once a given equilibrium stuation has been reached, the other equilibrium situations are precluded. In view of all this, our model does take "past history" into account in a formal or abstract way.

Although there is not a unique equilibrium situation, we can indicate the general price tendency: the price tends to settle at a level immediately above the entry-preventing price of the least efficient firms which it is to the advantage of the largest and most efficient firms to let live.

The elements of price determination are the following: (a) the absolute size of the market; (b) the elasticity of demand; (c) the technologies; and (d) the price of the variable factors and of machines which, together with the technologies, determine the total average cost of the firms.

Oligopoly and competition

We have had occasion to note earlier that the large firms do not stand to gain by raising the price even when demand is rigid. The reason is that this would induce new firms to enter or existing firms to set up new establishments.[16] In other words, demand can also be rigid for prices that are immediately higher than the equilibrium price. This cannot happen in the case of pure monopoly.[17] The reason is that in a situation of oligopoly the main purpose of the large firms, which control the price, is to keep new firms out. In this sense Andrews is quite right when he drives home the idea that businessmen, while generally in a position to fix the price — which they could not do under competition — have a narrow zone of discretion, just because they are afraid that firms operating in other markets or new firms may invade their market or that existing ones may expand. Businessmen worry much more about the reactions of existing or potential rivals than about those of consumers.

If this is so, then we may well ask how the oligopolistic situation which we have described differs from competition. Wherein consists the market power of the large oligopolistic firms and what are its consequences?

We shall see that no really satisfactory answer can be given with reference to the equilibrium position. The question can be

---

[16] If the firms capable of modifying the price do not raise it when the elasticity of demand is equal to or less than unity, they appear not to be maximizing profit in the sense of marginal analysis. This type of analysis gives us the formula $p - \dfrac{p}{\eta} = m$, from which it is easy to see that, assuming $\eta \lessgtr 1$, equilibrium is impossible. However, this simply means that such a formula, worked out with reference to the case of pure monopoly, is inapplicable in the case of oligopoly.

[17] In actual fact, it probably happens very often that demand is rigid at prices above the equilibrium level. In this context we may recall that Marshall observed that "habits which have once grown up around the use of a commodity while its price is low are not quickly abandoned when its price rises again" (*Principles*, Appendix H, pgh. 3) — that is, the demand schedule becomes more rigid. What Marshall alludes to is nothing but the microeconomic aspect of the problem which Modigliani discusses, with reference to a community's propensity to consume, in his well-known study on the consumption function: Modigliani, "Fluctuations in the Saving-Income Ratio," *Studies in Income and Wealth*, XI (National Bureau of Economic Research, 1949), part 5.

answered only in dynamic terms, that is, after having studied cost and price changes. All we can say at present is this: (1) In the circumstances of our model perfect competition is structurally impossible. (2) The profit rate of the medium and large firms is well above the minimum rate, and this high rate cannot be eliminated. A new large firm attracted by the high profit rate could not achieve it and, to boot, would cause losses to all firms. The alternative to a price yielding high profits to large firms is not a price which equals cost, but sheer chaos.

In competition, too, firms can enjoy above-minimum profits, but with a difference: under competition such profits are due to frictions and are transitory; under oligopoly they are structural and permanent. We might speak of partial or sectional monopoly profits earned by large and medium firms in comparison with small ones. We might also say that the larger profits are due to the greater efficiency of those firms. But we would have to add at once that their greater efficiency rests on different techniques and not on any exceptional ability of management.[18]

At this point we have to make a brief digression into the nature and the degree of realism of the different concepts of competition, especially in neoclassical and classical theory.

The neoclassical economists' perfect competition has never existed anywhere. The static hypothesis and the application of marginal analysis within it led the neoclassical school to ascribe to competition certain characteristics (in particular, perfect homogeneity of goods, horizontal demand curve for the individual firm) which severely limit the realism of the concept.

The classical economists' concept of competition, especially Ricardo's, is very different. Its principal distinguishing feature is ease of entry. As long as the entry of new firms is easy, no producer can raise prices, and, except for a short time, none can earn above-normal profits.[19] The classical concept (which we shall

---

[18] If anything, this would be the ability of the men who made the firms as great as they are; but in the case of today's established concerns, we would most often have to go to the graveyard if we wanted to pay homage to any such ability.

[19] A concept rather like the classical one was developed by Alberto Breglia in *Reddito sociale* (Rome, 1951). He considers the conditions of entry to be the fundamental object of study in the theory of market forms.

have occasion to discuss again later) refers to conditions which might be considered "dynamic": competition is not so much a situation as a *process*. For the purposes of certain types of analysis, the classical concept is preferable because, although it is less rigorous than the neoclassical one, it is much more realistic.

To mark the distinction between the two concepts, we shall call the first "neoclassical" or "perfect" competition and the second, "classical" competition or, simply, competition.

Differentiated oligopoly

So far we have assumed, among other things, that consumers have no preferences for the products of particular firms.[20] Thus we excluded those market imperfections which many economists regard as the principal source of the degree of monopoly. Our purpose was to make it plain that a certain degree of monopoly[21] is a congenital feature of the technical structure of concentrated industries, quite apart from the consumers' preferences or lack of knowledge and from the producers' uncertainty.[22] But all these factors are characteristic of differentiated oligopoly, and chief among them is the preference of consumers for the products of certain firms, these products being, or seeming to the consumers to be, different from those of other firms.

Differentiated oligopoly is often found in the industries producing consumer goods, and very often in trade. In trade, however, discontinuities of organizational methods may easily create situations rather like concentrated oligopoly. Indeed, the "jumps" may be quite as large as in industry. The grocer who supplies the inhabitants of a small district is economically farther away from — though imperfectly competing with — the great chain stores than is a small foundry from the giant iron and steel concern.

However, the kinship between the two types of oligopoly has other and more interesting aspects. In concentrated oligopoly,

---

[20] The assumption was either that the demand curve for each separate firm was horizontal or that the degree of monopoly in Rothschild's sense was zero ("The Degree of Monopoly," *Economica*, February 1942, pp. 24–39).

[21] The precise meaning of this expression will be discussed in Chapter 4.

[22] And quite apart, also, from tariff protection, deficiencies of the law, or other "artificial" elements.

technology creates *external* barriers between each group of firms and its potential competitors. In differentiated oligopoly, the situation seems to be different in that the barriers due to product differentiation are *internal* — they lie within each group of firms. Are there also external barriers? In a situation of concentrated oligopoly, these are jointly determined by technology and the size of the market. Similar barriers exist in a situation of differentiated oligopoly, where they are determined by the selling costs involved in acquiring an adequate circle of customers.[23]

These "installation" selling costs are comparable with fixed costs. In some markets fairly high initial expenditures have to be incurred not only to build up a sales organization capable of competing with that of existing firms, but also to make the product or products known and to gain the confidence of potential customers. These expenditures have to be sustained for a relatively long time, during which sales proceeds may be less than total cost.[24]

The higher the initial selling expenditure, the larger may be the circle of customers. But the relationship between the two is obviously not a simple one, and it would be absurd to try and represent it by a curve. The obstacle which impedes the entry of new firms and creates a situation of oligopoly for the whole group resides not so much in the difficulty of finding funds for the initial selling expenditure as in the difficulty of acquiring enough customers for sales receipts to cover not only current production cost but, in time, the installation expenditure as well. The discontinuity which obliges the entrepreneur to make sure of sufficient outlets derives not only from fixed technical costs but also from fixed installation costs; it arises from the fact that, if initial selling expenditures are made in small doses, they simply do not serve their purpose.

Hence there are external barriers also in differentiated oligopoly, and they are conditioned by the internal barriers due to consumer preferences, which create discontinuities similar in effect to technical discontinuities. To "produce" a certain group of buyers, the potential competitors must incur expenses which

[23] See Sraffa, "The Laws of Returns under Competitive Conditions," p. 549.
[24] See Andrews, chap. 5, n. 5.

cannot be divided into small amounts, and these expenses cannot be viewed in isolation but must be considered in relation to the anticipated number of customers. Anticipations of this kind are bound to be exceedingly uncertain, and the uncertainty increases the obstacles to the entry of potential rivals.

In our analysis of concentrated oligopoly, we neglected the market imperfections which are characteristic of differentiated oligopoly. We did so in order to emphasize the effects of technological discontinuities. But in reality these imperfections are often superimposed on the latter effects, thereby accentuating the degree of monopoly.

In its turn, product differentiation often entails different technologies, and different technologies imply quality differences in similar products. The two types of oligopoly[25] may thus be superimposed on each other for technological reasons as well.[26] Since we admit the validity (though not necessarily the solutions) of the problems examined by the theoreticians of imperfect competition — problems dealing principally with product differentiation and uncertainty — we may conclude that our own analysis is not in contradiction with theirs but complementary to it.

Finally, there is yet another category of barriers which may operate externally or internally in any given industry and which

[25] Industries typically in conditions of concentrated oligopoly include many of those producing major producer goods, such as iron and steel, chemical raw materials, electricity, oil, cement (see Introduction); non-durable consumer goods, such as textiles, tires, canned foods, soft drinks, and cigarettes, are often produced in conditions of differentiated oligopoly; and "mixed" oligopoly (concentration *cum* differentiation) is typical of some of the major industries producing consumer durables, such as automobiles, typewriters, refrigerators, radio and television sets. Competitive or quasi-competitive conditions can be observed in industries producing nondurable consumer goods and in subsidiary and satellite activities (see Introduction), provided concentration is low and differentiation unimportant.

[26] This observation, which it would be interesting to follow up, was suggested to me by Professor Siro Lombardini. I should like to avail myself of this opportunity to express my gratitude to him for his comments and suggestions after perusal of the first edition of this book (1956). As a result, the work is much improved, particularly in the following places: Chapter 2 (section on "Criteria and Assumptions of the Model"), Chapter 3 ("The Rationale of the Full-Cost Principle"), Chapter 4 ("The Validity of the Marginalist Principle"), Chapter 7 ("A Three-Sector Model").

is connected with technological barriers. These are the barriers created by patents and special technical methods requiring highly skilled workers or technicians, whose number is limited and cannot be increased rapidly. Here, too, the effects of these barriers are superimposed on those of the others. All in all, though, the main barriers are the technological ones and those deriving from installation selling expenditures. The two may, of course, be combined in different ways according to the market. Their joint restrictive effect on the entry of new firms can be summarized by saying that, by imposing relatively high initial investment and a relatively large initial size on potential competitors, they make it necessary for the entrants to have to count from the outset on a relatively large volume of sales. Ultimately, the barrier lies in the size of the market itself.

III

Price and Cost Variations

Is the preceding analysis in contradiction with the full-cost principle? If none of the data changed over time, the price-fixing procedure of entrepreneurs would lose any purpose it may have had originally. The price would remain where it is and the oligopolists would soon find it absurd — if they had not already found it tiresome — to go through the motions of determining a price which simply is what it is and which indeed, if the preceding analysis is correct, is "fixed" by forces over which the individual oligopolist has only partial control. But price fixing ceases to be absurd if it is assumed that the data vary. Let us look more closely into this.

The rationale of the full-cost principle

If the cost elements vary, the price must change. In the absence of a simple and universally applicable principle for arriving at a new equilibrium price — that is, at a price which, in the changed situation, is acceptable to all firms — the pattern of the whole industry (or of the whole group of firms) would be disrupted. There would be no way out of the ensuing chaos except at the cost of serious difficulties and losses, since oligopoly lacks those mechanisms of *continuous* adjustment which are an inherent feature of competition. We have to ask, then, what price changes a cost change entails.

The new price must again lead to an equilibrium situation: it must be a price which is acceptable to all existing firms and does not attract new ones. At the new price, the profit rates must be the same, or nearly the same, as those established in the previous equilibrium situation.

Let us see whether the new price can be determined by the formula

$$p = v + qv, \qquad\qquad (3.1)$$

or, more precisely,

$$p = v + q'v + q''v,$$

where

$$q'v = k/x$$

and

$$q''v = g.$$

In the short run, fixed cost, k, is not subject to much change. The salaries of the technical and executive staff may change, but not the depreciation allowance (unless the price of plant and machinery undergoes a very marked change). Hence k/x varies only with output, x. Generally speaking, at given techniques and output, variable cost, v, changes in the short run with the prices of the variable factors. Let us see, then, what help we can get from the full-cost formula when direct cost varies.

The simplest case is that of differentiated oligopoly in a market where all firms have almost equal market shares, use the same or very similar techniques, and have approximately the same average costs. Let us suppose that in such a market the demand schedule shifts, without changing its shape, when prices change.

If v increases and the price is raised in proportion to q which is kept constant, the new margin qv — provided that k/x does not vary — leads to higher unit profits than before and hence to a profit rate higher than the equilibrium rate. Conversely, if v diminishes and the price is similarly reduced at constant q, the new margin leads to a profit rate below the equilibrium rate. Consequently, and always on the assumption that k/x remains constant, the formula $p = v + qv$ needs to be corrected. When v rises, the coefficient q needs to be reduced somewhat, and when v falls, q must be raised. In this manner the previous equilibrium rate of profit can be reproduced.

Thus the simple formula (3.1) cannot be applied automatically. The price which implies the same profit rate is defined by the slightly more complex formula[1] we used for calculating the minimum profit rate:

$$p = (k/x + v)(1 + r) \qquad (3.2)$$

This equation also expresses the full-cost principle, but in a somewhat different manner. We shall have to distinguish two full-cost criteria, one of which is expressed by the formula (3.1) and the other by (3.2).

On our simplifying assumptions, the second formula allows us to calculate the new equilibrium price with more precision. However, if the changes in v are very small, the first and simpler formula can be applied almost automatically. The problem becomes more complicated in the case of concentrated oligopoly, where firms use different techniques. When direct cost varies because of changes in the prices of the variable factors, neither formula yields a single price because the different firms have different average costs. Yet the new price must be a single price.

The difficulty can be overcome if we assume, as before, that the price is fixed by the large firms, according to the first or the second of the two full-cost criteria. The new price will then approximately or precisely reproduce the same profit rate which the large firms earned in the preceding equilibrium situation. However, the new price may be more or less profitable for the smaller firms. If it is more profitable, new small or medium firms may be attracted to the market. As a result, the price will fall to the entry-preventing level, unless the large firms anticipate this development by lowering the price at once to the entry-preventing level which is below that indicated by formula (3.2). However, each of the large firms worries, above all, about the reactions of other firms of similar size (as large or only a little smaller) and normally tries to avoid the danger of an invasion of the market by other large firms or of a conflict with them. This danger is avoided by selecting a price which yields the same profit rate that all the large firms had in fact found acceptable

[1] See equation (2.2) above. This formula should be remembered when discussing pricing policy to achieve a target return on investment. See A.D.H. Kaplan, J. B. Dirlam, and R. F. Lanzilotti, *Pricing in Big Business — A Case Approach* (Washington, 1958), Part I, chap. 2.

in the previous situation. As a subordinate consideration, the firms which fix the price think also of the reactions of smaller firms.

In short, when the prices of the variable factors change, the direct costs of all firms change. In a situation of differentiated oligopoly, where firms apply the same or similar techniques, the new equilibrium price is calculated on the basis of the first full-cost formula and, if necessary, corrected by the second. In a situation of concentrated oligopoly not even the second, more precise, formula is good enough. Insofar as the price leaders also take into account the changes in the profit margins of smaller firms, they may, if necessary, introduce a further correction.

In differentiated oligopoly, where firms have similar costs and market shares, there are no price leaders. Nor is there any need for price leaders when the cost variations are relatively small, since in practice all the firms reach the same result in recalculating their own prices. This is the simplest case and it shows up the function of the full-cost principle quite plainly: it acts as a guide and enables the oligopolistic firms to achieve a new equilibrium quickly and without disturbance.

When the changes in direct cost are relatively small, the first formula generally is a good enough approximation for calculating the new equilibrium price. Cases of small cost changes are frequent and, therefore, firms tend to use the first formula, which has the additional advantages of simplicity and general applicability. If the changes in direct cost are considerable, or if there is a change in some other basic datum, such as size of market, elasticity of demand, technology, or the prices of fixed factors, then neither of the two formulas can be applied automatically. We shall discuss this in the following pages.

The main points can be summarized as follows. The analysis in the preceding chapter explains how equilibrium comes about in conditions of oligopoly. Once an equilibrium situation is established, each firm calculates what percentage of direct cost it must add to direct cost to arrive at the price. Subject to possible corrections, this percentage is then used as a basis for altering the price when the cost elements change. Here, in the cost changes, appears the rationale of the empirical principle followed by businessmen.

Variations in the determinants of equilibrium

We have discussed some consequences of cost changes affecting all firms. Now we go on to a systematic examination of the consequences for equilibrium of any changes which may occur in the various determinants of equilibrium: (1) the absolute size of the market, (2) the elasticity of demand, (3) technology, and (4) the prices of the factors of production.

Variations in the size of the market. By this we mean changes in the volume of sales not depending upon price changes. We may think of them as the results of shifts to the right or left of the demand schedule, without any change in shape. These variations are very important in practice. In a progressing economy, demand for many products often expands simply as a result of rising personal incomes, without any price changes. If prices are reduced, the increase in demand becomes proportionately bigger, at least during the period when the price reduction goes into effect.

What are the consequences of expanding demand for the equilibrium of the oligopolistic market?

The widening of the "economic space" may make room for (a) the entry of new firms, (b) the entry of large firms already established in another market, or (c) the expansion of existing firms in the same market through the setting up of new establishments.

The entry of large firms already established in other branches is relatively easier than the entry of new firms, especially insofar as the former possess large capital funds (primarily through self-financing), experienced technical teams, and a sales organization.[2] The chief obstacle to the entry of such firms is the size of the market: in an expanding market this obstacle loses some or all of its force. However, if the market expands or is expected to expand, the existing large firms may take steps to prevent the entry both of large firms from other branches and of small new firms; to

[2] H. H. Hines, "Effectiveness of 'Entry' by Already Established Firms," *Quarterly Journal of Economics*, February 1957, pp. 132–50.

do so they may reduce the price and set up new establishments which, although they cannot work at full capacity in the beginning, are expected to be fully utilized later as the market goes on expanding. It may also happen that the existing large firms will not find it worth their while to apply some known technique before the market has reached a certain size; the progressive expansion of the market may at some point make it profitable to apply that technique, even if the new plant cannot yet be operated at full capacity. What happens, then, when the market expands is that the existing large firms increase their capacity and eventually also their output. But if the market grows very rapidly, if the existing firms take too conservative a view of the market's ultimate potential, or if the price is considerably higher than the costs of the largest firms, then large firms from other branches will be induced to enter the market — even though they know that their entry is bound to provoke more or less violent adjustments and, in the end, result in a lower equilibrium price. The smaller firms, with their relatively higher costs, are eliminated or gradually leave the market. Generally speaking, therefore, growth of the market tends to increase the average size of firms and to lower the price (see p. 50).

However, when the market is already extensive and the rate of increase of demand is relatively low, and when there is not, as in the preceding case, any prospect of sizable economies of scale — in other words, in a mature and well-established industry — the large firms will not find it profitable to reduce prices because the expected widening of the economic space is slow and the threat of invasion by other firms — new or already established in other markets — is not serious. Nor will they find it profitable to raise prices because this would, in the short run, reduce the absolute size of the market and probably also reduce its rate of expansion in the long run. The best thing the large firms can do in these circumstances is to keep the price stable and to increase their productive capacity — that is, to invest, in proportion with the increase in demand. This amounts in effect to the large firms' trying to keep their market share.[3]

[3] In the branches in which this happens the capital/output ratio will tend to remain constant.

Variations in the elasticity of demand. Suppose that at a given price there is an increase in the elasticity of demand with respect to price rises. Nothing particular will happen; equilibrium remains unchanged. If, on the other hand, there is an appreciable rise in the elasticity of demand with respect to price reductions, new firms can enter the market. The situation is rather like the ones just described. The higher becomes the elasticity of demand and the more the economies of scale enjoyed by the large firms, the greater will be the increase in the average size of firms in the new equilibrium situation and the lower the new equilibrium price.

In practice, this will happen only if the increase in the elasticity of demand is plainly recognizable and patently large. Uncertainty about the elasticity of demand tends to perpetuate the existing equilibrium. For this reason, it is much more likely that the structure of the industry concerned and the equilibrium price will change as a result of a tendency of the market to expand independently of price changes, rather than of some doubtful change in the elasticity of demand. The first tendency translates itself into something tangible and measurable: the rate of increase of sales. If that rate of increase remains relatively constant over more than a short time, it can be extrapolated. Such extrapolation may be risky, but less so than hypothetical and in practice almost impossibly difficult calculations of changes in the elasticity of demand.

Changes in technology. Consider now cost variations due to technological change. Technical innovations reduce costs by reducing the production coefficients. Now, as Schumpeter observed, most innovations, and certainly major ones, entail construction of new plant and equipment.[4] This means that normally changes in the variable coefficients depend upon changes in so-called fixed capital.

An analysis of these and other cases of equilibrium situations resulting from a widening of the economic space would be of interest in the context of the gradual introduction of the Common Market in Europe. Apart from the possible consequences on concentration and prices in the industries of the participating countries, there is the particularly interesting further question of the conditions in which large firms in the different countries are more likely either to come to an agreement or to engage in a struggle.

[4] *Business Cycles,* I, 93.

If the new plant or equipment is within the reach of all firms, whatever their size, the cost reduction becomes general in a relatively short time and the equilibrium price must fall (according to the first full-cost criterion, possibly corrected by the second). But this is not so if only the largest firms can afford the new plant. Then the price remains unchanged; the cost reduction remains limited to these firms and they reap a higher profit than before. They can calculate a new margin q wider than the previous one, and this new q becomes the basis of any price changes these firms make in the case of general cost variations. The equilibrium price can change only if the new technology makes it profitable for the existing large firms or for new firms to start a price war, so as to eliminate the others and occupy their economic space. But this can happen only if the innovation is capable of reducing costs very considerably. Otherwise the costs of the struggle acts as a deterrent and the initial equilibrium will not be disturbed. The large firms will simply sit back and enjoy the greater profits they can get at the existing price, after the cost reduction.

Certain innovations are, in the nature of things, accessible only to certain types of firms and particularly to the larger firms. They include many mass production methods which are possible only in very large firms. But a firm can also take special steps, not necessarily connected with technical discontinuities, to make certain innovations inaccessible or less accessible to its competitors and thus avoid having to share the benefits of the innovations with them. The most obvious examples are patents, which protect new methods of production, and trademarks, which prevent imitation of certain qualitative features of the products.

However, the protection so acquired is precarious. A patent normally confers upon its holder a monopoly of a certain production method but not of production itself; legally, the protection period is long, but economically it does not last beyond a relatively short time. Other firms try to adopt similar methods and generally succeed, unless there are serious technical discontinuities or the innovation is altogether revolutionary. However, since success comes only after a certain interval, the initiators of the new production method reap extraordinary profits for some time.

The same can be said of changes in the quality of products.[5] Here, too, the firms try to differentiate their products in order to make extra profits and, in each period, these have the characteristics of monopoly profits. But again, if there are no objective obstacles due to technical discontinuities, there is no reason to think that rival firms cannot eventually achieve successful imitations. These monopoly profits, each considered in isolation, tend to disappear. Or, more precisely, each separate extraordinary profit due to some specific "quality" is transitory because competitors react by introducing a new quality in their turn; but the total flow of extraordinary profits of this kind may well continue, though subject to fluctuations, if the firms keep on introducing new changes in quality.

Changes in quality need not necessarily encounter the obstacles of technical discontinuity; on the other hand, the reactions of rival firms are bound to be slower than in the case of price competition. For these reasons, intense quality competition can be expected in conditions of differentiated oligopoly, to the detriment of price competition.

In the consumer-goods sector, quality competition is widely supported by advertising campaigns, which stress and make the most of each product's own peculiar characteristics and its difference from other products. Quality competition in the investment-goods sector, on the other hand, generally gets along with very little advertising. There has, in the nature of things, always been quality competition and product differentiation in the production of machines, which may be regarded as the principal investment goods. But, as we shall see, the question of the "quality" of machines has assumed particular importance in our times because of the growing importance of replacement investment.

In the course of time, quality competition displays itself in continuous, or almost continuous, qualitative changes, which themselves are the fruits of technical progress. Technical progress, of course, implies not only the production of new goods and the

---

[5] To take account of qualitative differences means considering the case which we have called differentiated oligopoly. See Henderson, "The Theory of Duopoly."

reduction of the technical coefficients per unit of any existing good, but also a qualitative improvement of goods at unchanged coefficients. In the case of consumer goods, quality improvements are a somewhat uncertain matter because they are judged subjectively by consumers who, furthermore, are influenced by advertising; but in the case of investment goods, they have a more precise meaning in that they raise the productive efficiency of every machine.[6]

Variations in factor prices. If costs decrease because of a fall in the prices of factors of production, all firms benefit and the price must fall. But there is a difference here between fixed factors and variable factors.

With fixed factors, the question is whether all plant and all machinery diminish in price. If the price fall affects only plant and machinery usable by none but the largest firms, the cost reduction remains limited to them and the price will not change. In any case, a fall in the price of plant and machinery has only a delayed effect on the costs of the firm, as and when the old machines come to be replaced by new ones. Even if the cost reduction is general, therefore, there will be a time lag until the price falls. By contrast, a fall in the price of variable factors has very rapid effects on cost. Such falls occur most often in the prices of factors used by firms of all sizes, and therefore lead to general cost reductions and eventually to a price reduction. (*Mutatis mutandis,* the same can be said of a rise in the price of variable factors.)

As we have seen, the full-cost principle can be applied easily and almost automatically only when the changes in variable factor prices are relatively small. The question remains to what extent it can be applied when these changes are considerable, as happens particularly at the height of a boom, in inflation, and in the early stages of a depression. (For our purposes, the case of

---

[6] While the notion of changes in productive efficiency is more precise than that of changes in the quality of consumer goods, it still presents conceptual difficulties which are among the thorniest in capital theory. Among the extremely scarce studies on this question, we may mention H. Staehle, "Technology, Utilization, and Productivity," *Bulletin de l'Institut International de Statistique,* 28th session, XXXIV, no. 4.

inflation is similar in effect to the case of a boom and we can omit it.)

Variations of direct cost and prices during prosperity

In a cyclical upswing, demand tends to expand even at constant or, indeed, rising prices. Demand schedules shift to the right. This makes room for the entry of new firms or for the opening up of new establishments by existing firms. A price rise proportional to the rise in the prices of variable factors does not cause sales to contract, but it may reduce their rate of increase. In that case existing firms will not suffer any actual loss, but they will be deprived of potential additional profit insofar as they miss an otherwise probable increase in permanent customers. Two ways are open to firms to avoid or at least reduce this loss of potential profit.

(1) If the firms' market power extends not only to the supply of their products but also to their demand for factors of production, and especially for the variable ones (labor and raw materials), the firms will tend to use that power to prevent a rise in the prices of these factors. This is anything but an unusual situation, and indeed, so far as labor is concerned, it is very frequent. The largest firms, which have the most power on product markets, also have the most power on the labor market; they are not only price leaders but also wage leaders.[7] This is one of the reasons why conflicts in the labor market tend to multiply in periods of boom and inflation.

(2) If the firms' market power in the demand for variable factors is not sufficient to prevent the latter from rising in price, the most profitable thing to do may be to contain the increase in the price of the products, by raising it less, in proportion, than the factor prices go up. This has the additional advantage of making it more difficult for new firms to enter a market, the expansion of which would otherwise make room for them.

Furthermore, the equilibrium price rises less than direct cost does, as we have seen, because of the relative constancy of k/x in the short run. We conclude that during prosperity the costing

[7] See Andrews, chap. 6.

margin q tends to fall. This tendency may disappear and ultimately yield to the opposite tendency in the final stage of the boom, when a general shortage of factors of production makes it difficult to set up new firms and when overtime pay swells the direct costs of many firms. In such conditions businessmen make hay while the sun shines; they raise product prices by as much as the prices of variable factors have risen, or more. The margin q may then become wider.

In any event, whenever the prices of variable factors increase, oligopolistic firms, and especially the price leaders, always increase the prices of the products. It is worth emphasizing that if these firms had taken account of probable consumer reactions — the elasticity of demand — they could in many cases have raised product prices even before the increase in factor prices because, as we have seen, there is reason to believe that the elasticity of demand is often smaller than unity at the market price. A price increase would then have caused an increase in the receipts of the firms. Unlike the case of monopoly, it is nevertheless perfectly possible that under oligopoly the price leaders do not, in fact, raise their prices until factor prices have increased.[8] The reason is that firms act with an eye not only to consumer reactions but also to the reactions of their actual or potential rivals. The increase in the prices of variable factors raises the costs of all firms (though not necessarily in the same proportion); after that increase, the price leaders can raise the price of the products without fearing the reactions of their rivals or the invasion of the market by new firms.

This state of affairs — and especially the fact that an equilibrium price is compatible with an elasticity of demand of less than unity — explains why it often happens in the oligopolistic sectors of modern industry that the leading firms can, in a period of prosperity and sometimes even of recession, easily "shift" onto the consumer, through a price increase, such wage increases as they are unable to prevent. At first sight, both wage and price increases seem to depend on the market power of trade unions

---

[8] *Cf.* Galbraith's "unliquidated monopoly gains": "Market Structure and Stabilization Policy," *Review of Economics and Statistics,* no. 2 (1957), esp. pp. 128–9.

(which is greater in each industry as the degree of concentration is higher). On closer inspection, we see that an equally and perhaps more important factor is the market power which the largest firms enjoy in the sale of their products. It is futile to look for the "culprit" — in the last analysis, the structure of modern industry is itself "responsible" for price rises.

Variations of direct cost and prices during depression

In a depression, and especially in its early stages, demand ceases to rise or diminishes. Demand schedules shift to the left. Does the elasticity of demand with respect to price reductions then rise or fall?

This is a much debated and still open question. R. F. Harrod, for one, maintains that in depression demand becomes more elastic because:

With an expanding income [in a boom], a man may slip by imperceptible stages into careless habits. A contraction recalls him to his senses. He is loath to relinquish enjoyments to which he has become accustomed and immediately begins to cast about for means of meeting adversity with the least inconvenience to himself. That same force of habit, which in times of improvement tends to make him an imperfect buyer, reinforces his activity when it is a question of economizing. . . . [Therefore], once the slump has set in, demand becomes suddenly much more elastic.[9]

Others, including Galbraith[10] and Schumpeter,[11] say the exact opposite.

Harrod may be right as far as the demand for the products of separate firms is concerned — that "special" demand conditioned by market imperfections, which is discussed by the theorists of monopolistic competition and forms an essential element of differentiated oligopoly. But things are different when we consider the demand for the products of an industry, or "general" demand, which is what matters in the case of concentrated oligopoly.

Consider, first of all, durable consumer goods. Schumpeter is surely right in saying:

[9] "Imperfect Competition and the Trade Cycle," *Review of Economic Statistics,* no. 2 (1936), p. 87.

[10] "Monopoly Power and Price Rigidities," *Quarterly Journal of Economics,* May 1936.

[11] *Capitalism, Socialism, and Democracy* (New York, 1947).

People who in depression worry about their future are not likely to buy a new car even if the price were reduced by 25 percent, especially if the purchase is easily postponable and if the reduction induces expectations of further reductions.[12]

As regards durable and nondurable producer goods, we must remember that these are in joint demand. Since each of the firms using the various groups of capital goods demands them all, a price reduction for only one group has little effect. Especially in an uncertain situation, such as depression, firms will expand their demand for capital goods only if the prices of all of them, or at least of the most important ones, diminish, and appreciably so. In other words, demand for the various groups of capital goods will respond to price reductions if the prices of all or of the most important capital goods fall simultaneously;[13] but demand for each good in isolation is relatively inelastic and probably becomes more so during a depression with its enhanced uncertainty and risk.[14]

During depression, then, special demand tends to become more elastic in markets of differentiated oligopoly, and general demand tends to become less elastic in many important markets where concentrated oligopoly often prevails. In these circumstances, the best price policy for producers varies according to the characteristics of demand and to the market form.

Take first the case of *differentiated oligopoly*. For each oligopolist only the special demand for his own products is directly relevant. General demand affects him only indirectly.

If at least some oligopolists find that their special demand becomes considerably more elastic, each of them may find it profitable to try to attract some of the others' customers by reducing his price even more than would correspond to the reduction in direct cost. The margin q diminishes.

---

[12] *Ibid.*, p. 95. See also *Business Cycles*, p. 539. Galbraith, in his 1936 article in the *Quarterly Journal of Economics*, expresses himself in a similar vein.

[13] See W. Adams, "The Steel Industry," *The Structure of American Industry*, pp. 175–7; S. Nelson, W. G. Keim, E. Mason, *Price Behavior and Business Policies*, Temporary National Economic Committee, Monograph No. 1 (1940), p. 51.

[14] If there is more uncertainty about the possible changes in the elasticity of demand with respect to price decreases, the result is much the same as when firms definitely believe demand to be rigid.

This may lead to the disappearance of net profit or even to a failure to recover fixed cost. However, in the short run it is possible to operate without covering fixed cost and the price would then tend to equal variable cost. Only if the price falls below that level (which we have called the elimination level) does the single firm suspend production and go out of business.

This is, in substance, a situation which Marshall envisaged. He thought that in such a situation not only do profits disappear but that fixed cost can be covered only if the producers act in some kind of common agreement, by a "code of trade morality which condemns the action of anyone who 'spoils the market' by being too ready to accept a price that does little more than cover the prime cost of his goods, and allows but little on account of his general expenses." [15] If the oligopolists really acted in common accord, they would never, even when a price reduction is advisable, go so far as to reduce the price to the extent of covering "little more than prime cost" — that is, to eliminate, or almost

---

[15] *Principles,* Book V, chap. 5, pgh. 6. It will easily be seen that the situation described by Marshall is fully compatible with oligopoly, but neither with perfect (neoclassical) competition nor, strictly speaking, with classical competition. Under perfect competition, the price is theoretically independent of the individual producer's action; it coincides with the marginal (direct) cost of each firm and ruins none of them, because in normal conditions the firm's marginal (direct) cost coincides with its minimum average cost or else exceeds it (according as the firm's size is equal to or greater than optimum size). Since, in any case, marginal cost is not lower than average cost, all costs are covered — both fixed and variable, whether marginal or average — and there is a profit as well. If the price falls below minimum average cost, no firm can do anything about it. No amount of moral condemnation can prevent it. Such price falls are not infrequent, for example, in agriculture.

However, Marshall's observations, far from being irrelevant, are very realistic, although they refer to an oligopoly situation and not to competition. This was, incidentally, pointed out also by Steindl and Wolfe (Steindl, *Small and Big Business,* p. 2n; Wolfe, "The Problem of Oligopoly," p. 181). Sraffa was right in maintaining that Marshall's theory of the firm, insofar as it sets out to explain price formation under competition, suffers from an incurable contradiction between formal consistency and realism. But, this being so, the point is to discover to what market forms that theory's formal consistency applies. It may well be that much of it can be salvaged or at least used in the construction of a theory of oligopoly or, more precisely, a theory of differentiated oligopoly. There remains the fact, of course, that Marshall's theory of the firm is incompatible with his own theories, for example, of the returns of factors of production. From the formal aspect, these latter theories presuppose competition.

eliminate, the margin q; indeed, since general demand becomes more rigid with respect to price reductions, the best measure to take would be to hold the price steady or to reduce it less than by the amount of the fall in direct cost. But if there are a good many firms, as often happens in differentiated oligopoly, then effective common action is difficult; in that case the simplest rule, which all firms can adopt without further ado, is to apply the first formula of the full-cost principle (that is, to reduce the price in proportion to direct cost, without changing the margin q), even if this means that fixed average cost is less than fully covered and unit profits fall. Marshall's "moral condemnation," as has been observed, implies tacit agreement among the entrepreneurs; during a depression the common accord is precisely to keep q unchanged.

In *monopoly*, by contrast, the producer has no existing or potential rivals to fear and produces a good for which there are no direct substitutes. If general demand (which alone is relevant here) becomes more rigid with respect not only to reductions but also to increases in price, it is to the monopolist's advantage to do more than to keep the price unchanged: it is profitable for him to raise it. What happens is that, with contracting output, average fixed cost (k/x) rises and, if the monopolist is in a position to raise the price, it is expedient for him to do so in order to avoid the losses or curtailment of profit entailed by the rise of k/x. The margin q increases markedly.

In *concentrated oligopoly*, where the ability to control prices is vested in one or a few firms, the margin q does not remain unchanged, as it does in differentiated oligopoly. The margin widens, but less so than in the case of monopoly. The dominant firms have more market power than any one firm enjoys under differentiated oligopoly, and they can, therefore, reduce the price by less than the fall in direct cost; but their market power is not strong enough to keep the price unchanged. There are limits to the extent to which the margin q can widen. If that margin ever became appreciably larger than that prevailing in other industries, there would be a strong temptation for firms in the other industries — and especially for large and financially powerful firms — to invade that particular market, which looks like an island of profits in the midst of a mounting flood of losses. Moreover, an excessive difference between price and cost might attract so many small firms that a diminution of the price becomes inevitable. The new price fixed by the dominant firms must, therefore, be such that there is not too much temptation for outsiders to enter the market, nor for the existing firms to break the group's discipline, whether or not it rests on a formal agreement. In short, the new price must always tend toward the equilibrium price, as determined by the fundamental equilibrium conditions of oligopoly (Chapter 2). The margin between price and direct cost cannot diverge too much from the normal margin.

However, in markets where concentration is very high and the obstacles (especially the technological obstacles) to the entry of new firms are considerable, a situation rather like that described for the case of monopoly may arise during mild recessions. If demand is rigid with respect to price increases, the contraction of sales and the consequent increase in average total cost make it profitable to raise the price, and the margin q increases.[16]

We have seen, when discussing differentiated oligopoly, that a considerable increase in the elasticity of special demand may make it profitable for some firms to start a price war as an alternative to the application of the full-cost principle by common accord. In that case the margin q diminishes and, in the limiting

---

[16] This apparently strange phenomenon, which seems to turn the "law of demand and supply" upside down, can occasionally be found even in the interwar period. After the Second World War, cases of this kind began to multiply, and during the 1957–58 recession in the United States they became so frequent as to attract much attention among economists. This is the much debated paradox of "recession with inflation." It should be noted that, in addition to the process discussed in this section, the 1957–58 recession was characterized also by the process described in the preceding section: despite the recession, which was mild, wages increased in many branches and raised variable cost. See Galbraith, "Market Structure and Stabilization Policy," and J. M. Blair, "Administered Prices: A Phenomenon in Search of a Theory," *American Economic Review*, May 1959, pp. 431–50, esp. pp. 435–8.

Save for minor modifications, the observations in the text were already contained in the 1956 Italian edition of this book; they seem to have been confirmed by the price movements in oligopolistic markets during the 1957–58 recession.

case, disappears. Price wars may take place also in concentrated-oligopoly markets where, for obvious reasons, they are even more ruinous. Therefore, if it is unlikely that a price war will seem advisable during a depression in the case of differentiated oligopoly, it is even more unlikely in that of concentrated oligopoly.

Neglecting the possibility of a price war, we can therefore conclude that during a depression the margin q tends to remain unchanged under differentiated oligopoly and tends to rise under monopoly and concentrated oligopoly, but less so in the latter case where the price leaders have good reason to contain the increase in the margin within fairly narrow limits.

Large firms and the prices of variable factors of production

We have so far assumed that the data which determine equilibrium in oligopoly are independent of the action of individual firms. But is this assumption justified in all cases? The answer is no, especially as regards direct cost.

As we have seen, the large firms are normally in a position to influence not only the prices of finished products but also those of the factors of production and more especially those of variable factors. However paradoxical it may appear, the largest oligopolistic firms, which also possess oligopsonistic power in the market for variable factors of production, have an interest in keeping these factor prices stable during a depression. The reason is as follows. We have seen that, except for monopoly and special cases of concentrated oligopoly, firms try to keep the margin q approximately stable. Now, with a constant q, prices can be maintained—and the losses due to depression reduced—in the measure to which the prices of variable factors are also kept stable.

A numerical example may serve to dispel any doubts. Let us say that the normal volume of sales is 100, fixed cost 200, direct cost per unit 10, and the margin q equal to 32 percent. The price is then 13.2. Suppose that depression causes sales to fall from 100 to 50 units. At various levels of direct cost and at constant q, prices and profits (or losses) are as shown in the first tabulation below. It is evident that the less the direct cost and price diminish, the larger will be the net profit, or the smaller the loss.

x	k	k/x_n	k/x	v	$p = v + qv$	Profit	Loss
100	200	2	2	10	13.2	120	—
50	200	2	4	10	13.2	—	40
50	200	2	4	9	11.9	—	55
50	200	2	4	8	10.6	—	70

In this example we have assumed a constant margin q, which implies that the firm which fixes the price applies the first full-cost criterion.

Slightly different results are obtained if we suppose that the firm adopts the second, and more precise, criterion. In that case it is not the margin q which remains constant, but the profit rate r (always with reference to the normal volume of sales). If r is 10 percent, prices and profits (or losses) are as shown in the tabulation below.

x	k	k/x_n	k/x	v	$p = (k/x_n + v)(1 + r)$	Profit	Loss
100	200	2	2	10	13.2	120	—
50	200	2	4	10	13.2	—	40
50	200	2	4	9	12.1	—	45
50	200	2	4	8	11.0	—	50

Here, too, losses are smaller when direct cost decreases less.

The argument holds if: (1) demand becomes very rigid during a depression; (2) the oligopolists have oligopsonistic power in the market for variable factors of production; and (3) the oligopolists do not depart too much from the full-cost principle in either of its two formulations. Condition (1) is present in many important cases during the first phase of depression; conditions (2) and (3) can reasonably be expected in markets which display a considerable degree of concentration and which are not completely upset by the depression.

Insofar as any oligopolistic firm has the power to influence the prices of variable factors—that is, principally, of raw materials and labor—it will therefore be in the firm's interest not to depress these prices.[17] The ideal way of controlling the price of raw mate-

[17] In the case of industries where the turnover of funds is such that receipts come in at long intervals while outlays for variable factors have to be made at short intervals, it may happen that oligopolists have less, or no, interest in keeping factor prices stable. The reason is that lower factor prices would reduce the firms' cash requirements which, during the long intervals between receipts, may need to be covered by bank loans.

rials is to control their production, and this becomes possible through vertical integration.

For the integrated firm, the price of raw materials becomes purely a bookkeeping matter, but for the other firms it is a real price. During a depression, the integrated firm can maintain the price of the product by maintaining the price of the raw materials and so has an enormous advantage over nonintegrated firms. (Even in normal conditions the advantages are great. If the various firms follow the full-cost principle, the integrated firms completely dominate the price because they control one of its main determinants, the price of raw materials.)

In the labor market, the oligopolists' interest in keeping labor costs stable during a depression may in practice lead them to adopt a passive attitude toward trade unions, so that wages remain unchanged. However, this course is more likely to be followed by nonintegrated firms. Integrated firms can maintain sales prices by maintaining raw-materials "prices" — which is a much more convenient method since it entails no actual disbursement of money. (Wage reductions may become desirable when liquid funds are very scarce.)

In general, oligopsonistic power in the market for variable factors of production greatly reinforces oligopolistic power in the product market.

In a depression, then, the dominant firms in a market of concentrated oligopoly have two ways of salvaging what may be salvaged of profits or at least of keeping losses down. One way is to increase the margin q, by lowering the price of the product by less than corresponds to the fall in direct cost; the other is to keep the prices of variable factors stable. If a dominant firm is in a position to control these latter prices, it will prefer the second method and will especially try to maintain raw-materials prices. This method avoids the limitations implied by the other, as described in the preceding section. Consequently, maintenance of raw-materials prices may, up to a point, become a substitute for an increase in q. This margin may become narrower during a depression, even in highly concentrated oligopolistic markets.[18]

[18] A conspicuous illustration of our argument is furnished by the development of costs and prices in the American iron and steel industry during the

In conclusion, to explain the different behavior during the business cycle of prices and of the margin q, it is not enough to consider the market of individual products; it is also necessary to consider that of variable factors.

Great Depression. This industry is a textbook example of a highly concentrated oligopoly, where the largest firms also control the production of the major raw materials: iron ores and coke.

Sho-chieh Tsiang writes toward the end of his detailed investigation of this industry during the period 1923–37 (*The Variations of Real Wages and Profit Margins in Relation to the Trade Cycle*, London, 1947): "unlike the behaviour of profit margins in the manufacturing industries as a whole . . . gross profit margins here display a distinct positive correlation with the level of output" (p. 111). Further, "the apparent stability of prices of crude iron and steel . . . seems to be chiefly the result of the stability of their prime cost of production" (pp. 116–7). Tsiang calls "gross profit margin" what Kalecki calls "degree of monopoly" — which latter, as we shall see, can easily be translated into terms of q. The gross profit margin and q vary in the same direction.

Richard Ruggles ("The Nature of Price Flexibility and the Determinants of Relative Price Changes in the Economy," in *Business Concentration and Price Policy*, Princeton, 1955, p. 483, also pp. 477–8) has assembled figures which show that from 1929 to 1931 direct average cost in the iron and steel industry fell by only 5 percent and the "price" (average money value) of the products by 8 percent (during the same period, the wholesale price index fell by 24 percent).

Neither Tsiang nor Ruggles attempted any real explanation of these facts.

IV

Marginal Analysis and Oligopoly

We are now in a position to try and answer a question we raised in Chapter 1. We asked there whether marginal analysis provided a valid solution of the oligopoly problem. A further question is whether the solution of marginal analysis is in accord with our own.

The costing margin q *and elasticity of demand*

We have already seen that, at constant marginal cost $(m = v)$, the full-cost formula (first full-cost criterion),

$$p = v + qv \qquad \text{or} \qquad p - qv = v,$$

corresponds to the formula reached by marginal analysis,

$$p - \frac{p}{\eta} = v.$$

The costing margin q and the elasticity of demand η are formally linked by the simple relation,

$$qv = \frac{p}{\eta}$$

or

$$q = \frac{1}{\eta} \cdot \frac{p}{v}.$$

Since $p - (p/\eta)$ is marginal revenue, we could regard the expression $p - qv$ as another way of expressing marginal revenue and conclude that oligopolistic firms determine their prices on marginalist principles. Or we could say that the full-cost principle and the marginalist principle lead to the same result. But this would be begging the question. Let us go back to the determinants of q.

We have seen that q depends upon the same elements which

determine the price: q is a residual, not an active, element. Once a certain equilibrium price is established, firms calculate the margin q and use it as a guide in maintaining the equilibrium relationships in case of change in the basic data, especially in direct cost. Hence the margin q is determined by the forces which determine p — that is, the size of the market, the elasticity of general demand, technology, and the price of factors.

Now the elasticity of demand is only one of the elements which determine q. The concept of elasticity of demand might conceivably be stretched so as to include the other elements. But this would completely alter the concept of η and, what is worse, preclude the possibility of analyzing the factors which determine equilibrium in conditions of oligopoly.

Moreover, these factors operate in different ways depending on the assumptions we make about the initial structure of the industry (*crié par hasard*) and about the category of firms which initiate the equilibrating movements.

Let us work out a numerical example on the basis of the model presented in the second chapter. If equilibrium comes about at a price of 19.4, the values of q for the various categories of firms can be calculated on the basis of the formula, $q = \dfrac{p - v}{v}$, and are as follows:

Firms	Percent
Small	11.0
Medium	21.2
Large	38.6

To calculate q for the industry as a whole — we shall call this (q) — we can apply the formula $(q) = \dfrac{\Sigma px - \Sigma vx}{\Sigma vx}$. If (as in case I' 3 in Chapter 2) the structure of the industry is,

Firms	Output
47 small	4,700
4 medium	4,000
2 large	16,000
	24,700

the weighted average of q is 29.1 percent.

If, instead, with the *same* equilibrium price and the *same* elasticity of demand, the structure of the industry is (as in case II' 2b),

Firms	Output
7 small	700
0 medium	—
2 large (3 establ.)	24,000
	24,700

then the weighted average of q becomes 37.6 percent.

This example shows that it is impossible to assimilate η to q: we now have two situations with equal elasticity of demand and equal price, but different distribution of firms, and as a result the margins q, for the industry as a whole, are significantly different in the two cases. Thus neither the industry's nor the individual oligopolistic firm's margin q can be resolved into η: q is the resultant of a conglomeration of forces, not simply of the elasticity of demand.[1]

The validity of the marginalist principle

Are we, then, to conclude that the marginalist principle, while formally correct, cannot explain equilibrium in conditions of oligopoly? Is it wrong to maintain that oligopolistic firms tend to maximize profit along the lines indicated by the marginalist principle? The answer to both questions is yes, but it needs to be properly qualified.

The marginalist analysis applies to maximization and minimization problems certain principles of differential calculus; this presupposes the assumption of continuous variations in the quantities under consideration. In the theory of the firm and the theory of market forms, marginalist principles are applied on the assumption of continuous variations in technical coefficients and

---

[1] And yet an economist as distinguished as W. Leontief has done just this in an empirical study published in the *American Economic Review* in December 1940, "Elasticity of Demand Computed from Cost Data," pp. 814–17. Leontief calculated the elasticity of demand for the products of U. S. Steel Corporation (elasticity of special demand) on the basis of the marginal cost figures of that company from 1927 to 1938. His figures, however, do not really express the elasticity of special demand, but can be used to calculate the margin q, which has a much more complex economic meaning.

in demand. But we have seen that the first assumption does not, as a rule, correspond to the facts, especially in modern industry. As regards demand, a curve is imaginable in the abstract, but in the presence of large technological discontinuities we have to consider *finite* elasticity and the notion of a curve becomes somewhat questionable. We would, instead, get a line proceeding stepwise which does not lend itself to derivation; as a result, the concept of marginal revenue is, strictly speaking, inapplicable. Furthermore, in conditions of oligopoly each entrepreneur is far more concerned about the possible reactions of his rivals than about those of consumers, of which the elasticity of demand is an expression.

In our discussion of price determination under oligopoly (Chapter 2), we have seen that the elasticity of demand is by no means the most important determinant of equilibrium. The equilibrium price is compatible with an elasticity of demand equal to unity, or higher or lower than unity. It is true that for the sake of simplicity we have spoken of a demand curve whenever this did not prejudice the analysis, but even so we always stressed that the shape of the curve matters far less than its shifts.

During prosperity, demand grows while price remains constant or even increases; we might say that the demand curve shifts to the right and presumably changes its shape. But rather than following the changes in the shape of a problematical curve, oligopolists (and especially the major ones) have to face quite another problem: the most accurate possible determination of the rate of expansion of total demand. Extrapolation of a rate of increase is a risky affair and may lead to disappointments, but it is still a good deal less problematical than making guesses about the shape of the demand curve. During depression, oligopolists generally have good reason to expect demand to be very rigid. If this is so, it is of little import to them to know the precise shape of the curve — which, moreover, does not stay put, at least until the bottom of the depression is reached, but tends to shift to the left and presumably to change its shape.

Things may be different for a monopolist or, more exactly, for a single producer who need not fear the invasion of his market

by other firms and who produces a good which is difficult to replace and demand for which is fairly stable. In that case the
elasticity of demand really does become the determinant element
of equilibrium and the monopolist will do well to calculate it as
best he can and to fix the price according to the marginalist principle.

There is, then, no marginalist solution for the oligopoly problem. Equality of marginal revenue and marginal cost is a solution
to the monopoly problem, not to the oligopoly problem where
the main analytical difficulty concerns the treatment of the
rivals' reactions. The objection against the marginalist solution
is neither that it is not formally correct nor that it is irrelevant.
The objection is that this solution is based on overly simple and, as
a rule, unrealistic assumptions and that, while having heuristic
value for monopoly, it is of no use in the problem of oligopoly.

Profit maximization

Marginal analysis rests on the assumption that each firm tries
to maximize its profits — an assumption which has more and
more insistently been called into question in recent years. The
problem of profit maximization is posed in static terms, or at any
rate with reference to the very short period. The analytical tools
are marginal revenue and marginal cost.

In our analysis we have not used these tools and we have distinguished two problems: the problem of the determination of the
equilibrium price in certain given technological and market conditions (Chapter 2) and the problem of price variations corresponding to changes in the data (Chapter 3). The latter we
have subdivided into two parts: price variations corresponding
to relatively small changes in direct cost, such as are the most
frequent in practice, and price variations corresponding to major
changes in direct cost and in the other data (we considered also
relatively small upward changes in demand).

In practice, the first problem — price determination — is relevant to an industry which is not yet firmly established or to one
which has undergone radical changes in technological or market
conditions, so that no universally acceptable price has as yet
emerged. The equilibrium price is an unknown magnitude toward

which the firms are groping. The object is to maximize profits in the long run, in the sense that each firm takes account not only, and not so much, of the reactions of consumers but also, and primarily, of such reactions as may be expected from existing and potential rivals in the given technological and market conditions. Each firm forgoes profit maximization in the short period if this is felt to prejudice profit maximization in the long period. The limits and conditions of profit maximization in the long period have been brought to light in the preceding analysis (see also Chapter 2, note 13).

The problem of price variations in response to variations in the equilibrium conditions is somewhat different. The object is still to maximize profit in the long period, but this can be achieved by the application of certain simple principles, as expressed in a full-cost formula. In the case of relatively small changes in direct cost, they can be applied mechanically; in the case of a major change in direct cost or other data, the formula has to be "corrected." Considered in isolation, these principles appear to contradict any assumption of profit maximization, but in the context of actual events the contradiction often disappears. In particular, the application of the second full-cost formula leads to price changes which tend to reproduce the previous rate of profit, which experience has shown to be compatible with equilibrium within the industry. This is what Cyert and March call a "satisfactory level of profit." [2]

In short, we have to distinguish between the decisions of day-to-day management and extraordinary decisions. Only the latter require an overall review of the situation; for the former, a partial review may well be sufficient to achieve the desired aim, and routine principles can safely be applied.

The firms' decisions may bear on price or on output. If demand expands, as is normal in a progressing economy, output may be expanded without altering the price; in a mature and fairly well-established industry, firms tend to expand output in proportion with demand and so keep their market share constant (see Chapter 3). Variations of this kind are very frequent in practice, and

[2] R. M. Cyert and J. G. March, "Organizational Factors in the Theory of Oligopoly," *Quarterly Journal of Economics,* February 1956, pp. 44–64.

this case can easily be combined with the equally frequent case of small variations in direct costs. Therefore, in mature industries, which constitute the majority in a highly developed economy, the firms' policy of aiming at a "satisfactory level of profit" and that of aiming at constant market shares are perfectly consistent.

The "degree of monopoly" and Kalecki's theorem of the distribution of national income

In traditional marginal analysis, the equilibrium price in a competitive system equals marginal cost; therefore, any divergence between price and marginal cost indicates the existence of a certain "degree of monopoly." This has been defined as the ratio of price less marginal cost to price, and it equals the inverse of the elasticity of demand:

$$\frac{p - m}{p} = \frac{1}{\eta}.$$

This definition of the degree of monopoly is highly unsatisfactory. First of all, in marginal analysis perfect competition and the resulting equality between price and marginal cost are logically admissible only on the assumption of particular marginal-cost functions, with marginal cost necessarily rising, at least beyond a certain point. With such functions the problem of covering fixed cost does not arise, since, at the point where the straight line representing price intersects the rising marginal cost curve, the price equals or exceeds total average cost and therefore covers fixed cost. But if marginal cost is represented by a straight horizontal line — as, in a case other than perfect competition, it may well be according to marginal analysis — then not all of the difference between price and marginal cost is net profit: at the equilibrium point, where marginal cost equals marginal revenue, part of that difference serves to cover fixed cost. Second, in terms of our own analysis, the margin q, which is also a type of divergence between price and marginal cost (assuming marginal cost to be constant and therefore identical with variable cost[3]), de-

[3] If $v = m$, we have $q = \dfrac{p - m}{m}$. Since the degree of monopoly, μ, equals $\dfrac{p - m}{p}$, we get $q = \mu \dfrac{p}{m}$.

pends on a whole set of factors and not on the elasticity of demand alone.

The truth is that the concept of the degree of monopoly as defined above suffers from the limitations of both marginal analysis and the static hypothesis,[4] and cannot properly be taken as a concrete measure of the degree of monopoly. A preferable alternative, for example, is that examined by Bain, who suggests considering the profit level as a possible index of the degree of monopoly.[5] But if we want to explore this question thoroughly, we have to say that in our time most industries are *structurally* noncompetitive and that this circumstance is reflected in all the economic magnitudes and their respective changes (prices, profits, wages, production, and employment). It follows that any single index of the degree of monopoly is bound to be unsatisfactory.

The question of the degree of monopoly defined in terms of marginal analysis was discussed at great length after Michael Kalecki presented his proposition that the degree of monopoly was one of the determinants of the distribution of national income and, in particular, of the share of manual labor.[6]

Let us consider for a moment what Kalecki says. According to him,

$$\frac{C + D + S}{T} = (\mu),$$

where C is aggregate net capitalistic income, D aggregate depreciation, S aggregate salaries, T aggregate turnover, and (μ)

---

[4] The same limitations apply to one of the most debated propositions of modern welfare economics, which is logically connected with the concept of the degree of monopoly. I have in mind the proposition that the optimum price for society is the price that equals marginal cost; if this price fails to cover fixed cost, then fixed cost must be covered by income taxes. The serious limitations of this view become evident as soon as we make a distinction between short-period and long-period marginal cost or consider the question of what method of financing the development of some particular productive activity is most advantageous for society as a whole.

[5] Provided that, in each individual case, the "accounting" rate of profit is corrected after careful analysis of the cost elements and the assets; see J. S. Bain, "The Profit Rate as Measure of Monopoly Power," *Quarterly Journal of Economics*, February 1941, pp. 271–93.

[6] "The Determinants of Distribution of National Income," *Econometrica*, April 1938.

a weighted average of the "degrees of monopoly" of all firms. (Kalecki takes variable cost to be constant and therefore equal to marginal cost.) The numerator is "gross capitalistic income" and is the larger, the larger is (μ). Since gross national income is the sum of "capitalistic income" and "labor income" (wages), it follows that the higher is (μ), the smaller is the wage share in national income. Kalecki's procedure in arriving at this equation is somewhat laborious.[7] A similar relation can be much more easily derived from the first full-cost formula: $p = v + qv$.

Variable cost, v, is the sum of average labor cost, w, and average raw-materials cost, a:

$$v = w + a.$$

Hence we get for the price:

$$p = w + a + q(w + a).$$

If we multiply all terms by the quantity of output, x, we get

$$px = wx + ax + q(wx + ax),$$

where wx and ax are total labor cost and total raw-materials cost.

This formula applies to the individual firm. In making the transition to all firms in all industries, we have to replace q by the weighted average (q); Σpx becomes gross industrial product, which we call Y_i; W is the total wage bill; and A is the cost of the aggregate input of raw materials. From our previous formula we derive

$$\frac{1}{1 + (q)} = \frac{W + A}{Y_i},$$

or

$$\frac{1}{1 + (q)} - \frac{A}{Y_i} = \frac{W}{Y_i}.$$

This expression corresponds to Kalecki's and can easily be translated into his terms. It says that the share of gross industrial product which goes to labor (W/Y_i) depends upon the margin

---

[7] He later reconsidered the question and arrived, by a different path, at a similar equation. See his *Theory of Economic Dynamics* (New York, 1954), Part I, chap. 2.

(q) and upon the share of raw materials in Y_i; the labor share declines when *(q)* and A/Y_i rise.

Kalecki holds that in a highly industrialized society gross industrial product is a fair approximation to gross national income.[8] The main purpose of his analysis is to explain the relative constancy over time of the wage share in British and United States national income. Since he finds that the degree of monopoly has been growing, he suggests that this relative constancy of the wage share may be explained by the decline in the relative prices of raw materials, which decline he regards as purely accidental.[9]

Kalecki's theorem has been criticized on various grounds, and most insistently on the following two:

(1) It is said to create the mistaken impression that not only profit but even the normal practice of covering fixed cost fall under the heading of "monopolistic exploitation."[10] Firms with different fixed plants may very well have different degrees of monopoly and yet earn the same profits; nor is it excluded that their profit rate may be low.[11]

(2) It is said to be tautological in that it defines the degree of monopoly in such a way that is must coincide with the sum of fixed cost and profit per unit of product;[12] it therefore does not explain the degree of monopoly but makes it by definition depend upon the difference between price and marginal cost. In Kaldor's words: "Unless the 'degree of monopoly' can be defined in terms of market relationships of some kind . . . and an attempt is made to demonstrate how these market relationships determine the relation between prices and costs, the theory does not provide a hypothesis which could be affirmed or refuted."[13]

---

[8] In *Theory of Economic Dynamics* Kalecki generalizes his theory to extend it to the whole gross product of the private sector (chap. 2, esp. p. 30).

[9] This last opinion will appear doubtful in the light of our subsequent remarks about the long-term rigidity of oligopolistic prices and about "privileged productions" (see Chapters 5 and 6).

[10] Andrews, *Manufacturing Business,* chap. 1.

[11] R. H. Whitman, "A Note on the Concept of 'Degree of Monopoly,'" *Economic Journal,* September 1941, pp. 261–9.

[12] F. Machlup, *The Political Economy of Monopoly* (Baltimore, 1952), chap. 12.

[13] N. Kaldor, "Alternative Theories of Distribution," *Review of Economic Studies,* no. 61 (1955–56), pp. 92–3.

The first point is well taken, as we have seen. To avoid sterile discussion, it is better to talk simply of the gross profit margin, without enquiring in what sense and to what extent it is the expression of any "degree of monopoly." The second objection may be valid as long as μ is not explained or, what amounts to the same thing, as long as it is explained with reference to an imaginary elasticity of demand for the whole economy.[14] But the objections do not hold if our above explanation of the margin q is acceptable. This explanation removes the tautology: the basic elements which we have examined are the determinants of q, and q in its turn determines the distribution of gross receipts among variable cost, fixed cost, and net profit.

[14] Kalecki, somewhat cautiously, made such a reference in his first article and dropped it in his later work; but there he defined the degree of monopoly in terms applicable only to markets with product and price differentiation, that is, to imperfect or differentiated oligopoly and not to concentrated oligopoly with homogeneous products.

V

Profit and Wage Tendencies

The British and American statistics examined by Kalecki show that in recent decades the degree of monopoly has gradually increased, and with it the margin q. However, this increase does not necessarily imply a corresponding rise in net profits per unit. The widening of the margin q may be due to an increase in average fixed cost — that is, to an increase in capital intensity, which in turn is conditioned by the growing mechanization of productive processes. This tendency is quite clearly perceptible and has been thoroughly studied by several writers.[1]

Unit profits

Is there reason to think that net unit profits have also gone up? The answer is uncertain. If such a tendency exists, it is a good deal less evident than the increase in average fixed cost. However, for highly concentrated industries, it would seem that the answer is in the affirmative. When discussing technological change (Chapter 3), we observed that the cost reductions due to technical innovations are translated into price reductions only if the innovations are accessible to all categories of firms. If this is not so, these cost reductions may lead to an increase in q, which then implies an increase in the net profit per unit of output. The likelihood of the occurrence of such circumstances increases with advancing concentration, since concentration accentuates the technical discontinuities which protect larger profits. The margin

[1] Maffeo Pantaleoni was the first to discuss it in the wider context of the progressive transformation of direct into overhead costs. See "Di alcuni fenomeni di dinamica economica," *Scritti varii di economia* (Rome, 1910) and *Erotemi di economia* (Bari, 1925), II, 100–106; or, in English, "Some Phenomena of Economic Dynamics," trans. S. d'Amico, *International Economic Papers* (1955), V, 41–51.

q may, of course, also widen when artificial obstacles are created against the entry of new firms, when a number of firms enter into monopolistic agreements, or when there is an increase in the market imperfections analyzed by the theorists of monopolistic competition.

At first sight there would seem to be no empirical evidence to support the presumption that net unit profits have been rising. The statistics show almost no exceptionally high profit rates, and indeed the largest companies (which, according to our analysis, ought to have the largest profits) seem to have profit rates below rather than above what is considered "normal"; the normal rate itself appears generally contained within rather modest limits and has certainly not risen.[2]

However, first of all, unit profits must be distinguished from the profit rate; and, second, we have to remember that the profit rates shown in the statistics are mostly those of corporations and are calculated either on equity or on total capital assets. These profit rates may be deceptive in that the exceptionally high profits which are or become stable — and which therefore are or become monopoly profits — disappear as such and are capitalized. It is the same thing that occurs with ground rent, which is capitalized on transfer of property: capitalization works to the benefit of those who own a particular piece of land during the period in which the process described by Ricardo takes place — if it takes place. Where, then, are exceptional profits capitalized and so made to disappear?

Capitalization may take place either in the stock exchange or in the balance sheet of the company earning the profits, or in both.[3] If it happens in the stock exchange, the current value of the shares durably exceeds their nominal value and the beneficiaries are those who own the shares during the period in which their value rises. If it happens in the company's balance sheet, the common methods of channeling extraordinary profits to the shareholders are the distribution of a scrip issue of shares and the preferential sale of shares at prices below market value. The

[2] W. L. Crum, *Corporate Size and Earning Power* (Cambridge, Mass., 1939).
[3] I am not here considering increases in profits and in the value of shares depending on inflationary processes.

capitalization of extraordinary profits puts the formal seal on the increase in value of the firm's material assets or its good will or both — good will being defined as the difference between the value at market prices of the firm's material assets and the value resulting from capitalization of the firm's net profit at the current rate of interest.[4]

The question of overcapitalization

In a 1952 essay, Harrod worked out his own theory of profit, which pays due attention to the problem of the capitalization of monopoly profits.[5] Indeed, he seems to regard this as a novel problem. But the works on cartels and trusts which were published around the turn of the century show that this problem had pride of place in all the debates, whether on theory or economic policy, about the new monopolistic formations.[6] The question which received most attention was that of "overcapitalization." This question, which is akin to that we raised above, deserves special mention.

It often happened, especially in those branches of production where concentration was most advanced, that the largest firms tried to gain complete control of certain industries. The "cost of struggle" at times appeared too high; yet it seemed advantageous to occupy with large plants the economic space hitherto occupied by small firms (see cases II' in Chapter 2). The large firms preferred to buy up the small firms rather than to incur the costs of struggle.

The funds required to buy out small firms frequently reached astronomical figures, since it was often a matter of buying a

[4] These observations obviously hold for any type of firm, whether or not it is a corporation. The good will (which in practice is often worth much more than the firm's material assets) may thus be regarded as capitalized monopoly profit. Note that the expression "monopoly profit" obviously excludes the popular notion of rapacious exploitation without corresponding cost. Most often good will, especially in small firms, is the fruit of hard honest work, by which the entrepreneur has gained his customers. The fact that certain market imperfections are inevitable (we may call them structural) does not make them any less imperfect and does not eliminate their consequences, however negative or even harmful these may be for society.

[5] "Theory of Profit," *Economic Essays.*

[6] This is another example of how important it is for the theoretical economist to study economic history.

whole slice of an industry. How could the large firms lay their hands on so much money? Various devices were applied through the stock exchanges and banks, and a whole new species of "promoters" grew up who were specialists, as it were, in the financial production of monopolies.[7] One of these devices was to sell shares at a value corresponding to the capitalization of the larger profits expected after the creation of the monopolistic combine. "Prices will not go up," the promoters hastened to proclaim in order to reassure the public. Higher profits would come exclusively from cost savings due to further concentration of firms.[8] Sometimes prices did go up later, contrary to these assurances, but more often they were left more or less unchanged. Sometimes they rose, but soon collapsed again because the whole operation failed.

It may be recalled that a number of economists lent their authority to arguments of this kind. They said that there was really no monopoly in the absence of a price rise and restriction of production. If such profits were obtained by cost savings rather than price rises, "everybody is happy" and these combines need not be branded as monopolistic.

We shall have occasion to return later to the consequences for employment and economic development due to this kind of price rigidity, that is, failure of prices to fall in accordance with cost reductions. Meanwhile, it is at once evident that this reasoning implies a static view of monopoly, such as was rightly and effectively criticized by Schumpeter. These profits were monopoly profits, even if they were due to cost savings and not to price rises.

Not infrequently the high hopes of the promoters proved to have been too optimistic. The market power they managed to conquer was not enough to produce the expected profits. Consequently, the anticipated capitalization of these profits proved excessive. But the shares had been sold and the companies had to pay dividends; even high unit profits did not ensure an appropriately high profit *rate*. Hence the protests, on the part of

[7] See G. J. Stigler, "Monopoly and Oligopoly by Merger," *American Economic Review,* Supplement, May 1950, p. 30.

[8] See case II' (2) in Chapter 2.

shareholders and others, against the corporation managers and hence the lively discussion of overcapitalization,[9] of diluted capital and fraud.[10]

If the operation succeeded, no protests were heard, but the fact remains that what was involved was capitalization of monopoly profits. The difference was simply that in the latter case things were done with discretion, and in the first case *avec trop d'élan*. In case of success, nothing was heard of any watering of stock; but part (and sometimes a large part) of the wine was monopolistic wine.

Wage increases

However, in oligopoly cost reductions are not necessarily translated into higher profits. They may be and often are translated into higher wages for the workers. This may be due to strong trade-union action, to government intervention, or to any combination of the two causes.[11]

In general, cost reductions may be translated into lower prices — which, in conditions of oligopoly, happens only when the cost reductions affect all types of firms (Chapter 3); into higher profits, at constant prices (Chapter 5); and into higher wages, at constant prices.

The cost reductions discussed above resulted from technological or organizational innovations. They may also result from a fall in factor prices. When the price of machines falls, it is their accessibility to various firms which is decisive: in the case of machines which only the largest firms can afford, the cost reduction tends to translate itself into higher profits. If there is a fall in the price of variable factors, the cost reduction tends to translate itself into lower prices, as we have argued earlier at

[9] See, for example, C. R. van Hise, *Concentration and Control* (New York, 1912), esp. pp. 28, 29, 115.

[10] Irving Fisher, when attending a meeting on trusts and combinations where overcapitalization was on the agenda, discussed it with admirable frankness and critical spirit; see *Proceedings of the National Conference on Trusts and Combinations, Chicago, October 1907*, National Civic Federation (New York, 1908), pp. 190–3. Marshall made some very interesting observations on this point in *Principles*, Book V, chap. 9, pgh. 2n.

[11] It may also happen as a result of "political" decisions on the part of the management of large oligopolistic firms. But that is another matter.

some length. But it may happen that the price of some variable factors falls while the price of others rises; for instance, raw-material prices may fall while wages rise. This is a case which deserves special attention. Lower raw-material prices may cause firms not to offer too much resistance to the trade unions' wage demands, and then the saving in the cost of raw materials may wholly or partly offset the wage increase so that direct cost ultimately remains unchanged or changes only a little. This case is similar to that discussed above (p. 76), where nominal wages do not contract during a depression because of the behavior of large oligopolistic firms and where the maintenance of wages makes it possible to maintain sales prices. This holds for non-integrated firms, or firms which do not control the production of the raw materials they employ. If raw-material prices sustain a heavy fall, the firms have no interest in depressing wages but can even let them rise, provided the recession is relatively mild.

Constant nominal wages mean growing real wages when the cost of living diminishes, as it is apt to do during a depression. But the workers employed in the oligopolistic industries where this happens do not normally experience a sudden rise in their standard of living. The wages in question are those per unit of output or hourly wages; but during a depression many workers are on short time (especially in heavy industries where concentration is, for technical reasons, more advanced than elsewhere and which, therefore, commonly display the market form of concentrated oligopoly). Furthermore, many workers are dismissed and many others are under threat of dismissal. The beneficial effects come later, when effective demand resumes its upward trend and production and employment expand again. However, during the boom the trade unions have the problem of defending the higher real wages because in that phase the mechanism which induces the large firms to keep wages up becomes inoperative.

Short-run price rigidity

In this context it may be useful to dwell for a moment on a question which has been the subject of lively controversy among economists. This is the question of price rigidity due to monopoly or oligopoly. The discussion turns principally on two main points: (1) the definition of price rigidity, which must be analytically satisfactory and usable in empirical investigations; (2) the consequences of price rigidity,[12] in particular for business cycles, employment, and economic development.

We must distinguish between long-run and short-run price rigidity. The first is relevant for problems of development and employment, the second for business cycles. The two concepts of rigidity are linked and, to some extent at least, long-run rigidity is the result of short-run rigidity. But they are not the same, as will become patent when we examine long-run rigidity in Chapter 6. This fact, though affecting problems of great interest to economists, has so far been neglected by them.

On the definition of short-run rigidity a certain measure of agreement has been reached. Assuming that industrial firms normally produce in conditions of constant direct cost, a number of economists, including Dunlop, Neal, Tsiang, Ruggles, and others, use Lerner's "degree of monopoly" — the ratio of price

[12] The discussion among statisticians began after the publication of an article by Gardiner Means, which appeared just at the worst moment of the Great Depression and eventually became incorporated into the official papers of the United States Senate (Senate Doc. No. 13, 74th Congress, 1st Session, 1935). Means argued, in agreement with neoclassical theory, that the rigidity of industrial prices seriously aggravated depression and unemployment. The discussion which this article provoked has its place not only in the history of economic thought, but it also entered into modern economic policy when President Roosevelt gave this opinion official authority in a message to Congress of April 29, 1938. This message contains a section entitled "The Decline of Competition and its Effects on Employment," where Means's thesis is condensed in the formula, "managed industrial prices mean fewer jobs"; see *The Public Papers and Addresses of Franklin D. Roosevelt,* compiled by S. I. Rosenman, VII (1938 vol.), 305.

Critical examination of the question and full bibliographic references may be found in the following: G. Haberler, *Prosperity and Depression,* United Nations (3rd ed., Lake Success, 1946), Part III, chap. 13; E. S. Mason, "Price Inflexibility," *Review of Economic Statistics,* no. 2 (1938), pp. 53–64; J. Dunlop, "Price Inflexibility and the Degree of Monopoly," *Quarterly Journal of Economics,* August 1939, pp. 522–3; Sho-chieh Tsiang, *The Variations of Real Wages,* chap. 5; A. C. Neal, *Industrial Concentration and Price Inflexibility,* American Council of Public Affairs, 1942; Ruggles, "The Nature of Price Flexibility and the Determinants of Relative Price Changes in the Economy." See also A. P. Lerner, "The Concept of Monopoly and the Measurement of Monopoly Power," *Review of Economic Studies,* June 1934, reprinted in Lerner, *Essays in Economic Analysis* (London, 1953).

minus direct cost to price — as a measure of short-run price rigidity. They define as rigid those prices which, in a depression, fall less, in proportion, than direct cost falls.[13] Their conclusions are based mainly on analyses of market behavior during the depression of 1929–34, and all except Tsiang found that price rigidity neither increased nor, indeed, was more marked in concentrated industries than elsewhere.

Ruggles, who takes full account of earlier work, observes:

> Generally speaking, the correspondence between the drop in direct costs and the drop in prices for the various (manufacturing) industries is quite close (p. 482).
>
> The major pattern of price behavior in the economy can be adequately explained in terms of factors other than industrial concentration (p. 488).

Tsiang was led to a different conclusion by his study of American manufacturing industry in the period 1919–37. He found that the gross profit margin, the variations of which correspond to those of q, for the whole of United States manufacturing varied irregularly: from 1919 to 1929 it varied in the cyclical sense (falling during the short but sharp depression of 1921 and rising during the following recovery); from 1929 to 1937, on the other hand, it varied in the opposite sense (rising during the great depression and falling during the subsequent recovery). All in all, over the whole period, the gross profit margin had a slight but persistent upward trend, which Tsiang interprets as a sign of some increase in (short-run) price rigidity.[14]

Contrary to what may appear at first sight, Tsiang's results can not only be reconciled with Ruggles' but also fit into our own analysis. In Chapter 3 we have seen that during a depression:

(1) The margin q generally remains unchanged in markets where differentiated oligopoly prevails, rises to a limited extent in markets with concentrated oligopoly, and rises more markedly in monopolistic markets.

(2) The margin q diminishes sharply in oligopolistic markets where a price war breaks out and remains unchanged or diminishes in concentrated oligopolistic markets where firms control variable factor prices.

[13] In this sense, rigidity can be measured directly by variations in the margin q, which, as we have seen, can easily be translated into terms of μ.

[14] Tsiang, *The Variations of Real Wages*, esp. pp. 73–6, 85.

Ruggles' analytical study of many manufacturing and mining industries and of commercial activities extends over two years only, from the top of the boom in 1929 to 1931, when the depression was well under way. He found that the margin q varied little or not at all. Tsiang considered *all* manufacturing industries over the period 1919–37; he found that between 1929 and 1931 the gross margin rose slightly (from 26.7 to 28.1 percent). This increase may be interpreted as a result of the algebraic summation of opposing changes of q in different industries. However, if we accept Ruggles' results, the cases in which q does not change or changes only a little are the most frequent.

During prosperity, our analysis in Chapter 3 has shown the margin q to be generally falling, while it tends to rise again at the peak of the boom. This conclusion agrees with the result of Tsiang's empirical study (Ruggles did not examine any upswing period). In the long or very long run, q has a rising trend, which has been interpreted as due to a rise in g (profit per unit) or in k/x (average fixed cost), or in both.[15] It is important to remember, however, that all the economists we have quoted implicitly assume that direct cost is independent of any action on the part of the firm. But, as we have seen, this assumption is inadmissible in conditions of concentrated oligopoly. It is true that Ruggles has some doubts on the matter:

Throughout the analysis up to this point, it has been implicitly assumed that when changes in direct costs agreed with changes in prices, it was not because the direct costs themselves were determined by prices. Should the causality run in the opposite direction, *i.e.* should direct costs be determined by prices . . . , the question of what determines prices would still remain open (p. 487).

Again, in a footnote on the same page, he says:

To the extent that differences in the behavior of the wage rate might be explained by differences in industrial concentration, . . . it is still possible that industrial concentration would in fact affect prices.

Ruggles does not go beyond these observations and leaves them unconnected. Our preceding analysis establishes the connection and furnishes an explanation. As regards the second ob-

[15] Apart from Tsiang, see also Kalecki, *Theory of Economic Dynamics*, p. 21.

servation, in particular, we may recall the conclusions of two important empirical studies on industrial wage structure, which appeared together in the *Quarterly Journal of Economics* in May 1950, although they had been submitted independently: the first is by A. M. Ross and W. Goldner, and the second, which is of more interest for our purposes, is by J. W. Garbarino. We quote from the latter study, but, on the points mentioned, the conclusions of the first are by and large the same. Garbarino writes:

The rank correlation coefficient for the relationship between the degree of concentration and changes in earnings is .67. . . . With the elimination of the Coke industry . . . the coefficient rises to .75 (p. 299).

And further:

Since the time period covered by the statistics includes a major [1929–33] and a minor [1937–38] depression period, the secular relationship found to exist between concentration and earnings might find its source in a failure of wages in this type of industry [oligopoly] to decline in depressions (p. 300).

These conclusions agree with our analysis in Chapter 3 and here. More than that, they confirm and illustrate it, and together with it provide valuable raw material — or even more on certain points — for the construction of a much needed modern wage theory.

If our analysis is correct, then there is no reason to believe either that prices need be rigid (in the sense indicated) in oligopolistic markets during a depression or that the coefficient q must increase. In general it does not change at all or changes very little. In monopolistic markets, on the other hand, prices do tend to be rigid.

Another definition relates price rigidity to the frequency of price changes. Rigidity is greater when prices change less often, when price variability over time is small. The hypothesis of a kinked demand curve implies a presumption that the variability of prices is small in oligopoly, and indeed smaller than in monopoly.[16] But we have seen that this hypothesis is not essential for an explanation of equilibrium under oligopoly and have

[16] G. Stigler, "The Kinky Oligopoly Demand Curve and Rigid Prices," *Journal of Political Economy*, 1947, reprinted in *Readings in Price Theory*, esp. pp. 420ff. See also above, p. 22.

worked out an independent explanation. It follows that the presumption of smaller variability of oligopolistic prices no longer stands. Indeed, Stigler, in the article which we have quoted and which was widely discussed in the United States, found that in actual fact oligopolistic prices are less rigid than monopolistic ones.

We have so far discussed short-run rigidity. However we define it, it has far less importance than long-run rigidity, to which we shall have occasion to return in connection with the effects of technical progress.

Part Two

THE DISTRIBUTION OF THE FRUITS
OF TECHNICAL PROGRESS

VI

The Mechanisms of Competition and Oligopoly

The analysis in Part One opens the way to a problem of fundamental importance: how are the fruits of technical progress distributed under different market forms, and what are the consequences of the manner of distribution on employment and economic development?

Let us briefly recall the views of the classical theorists, in particular those of Smith and Ricardo.

The classical theory

The classical economists assumed that competition was at work in most markets. Competition was inseparable from economic development and was a means of distributing the benefits of technical progress. Indeed, it was the ideal means from the point of view both of general welfare (the benefits were spread as widely as possible) and of economic development (competition actually promoted further development). The salient points of Ricardo's specific thesis were:

(1) Technical progress, which essentially consists in the introduction of new machinery, leads to a decrease in the costs of production.

(2) Through competition, the decrease in costs sooner or later results in a lowering of prices.

(3) During the transition stage, entrepreneurs reap "unusual profits," and the prospect of such profits induces them to adopt new production methods.

(4) Eventually, money profits return to normal levels and real profits increase because of the fall in the prices of consumer goods.

(5) Concerning wages, Ricardo usually worked with the simplifying assumptions that wages tend to be so low as to permit only the purchase of necessaries, such as food and clothing, and that real wages are constant, which means that nominal wages change in proportion to the prices of these goods. These prices tend to rise as a direct or indirect result of decreasing returns from land; hence nominal wages tend to rise correspondingly. Sometimes, when Ricardo wanted to be more realistic, he admitted that in a developing society, where capital is continually on the increase, the workers may have real wages above the minimum,[1] and also that, when the introduction of new machines causes consumer prices to fall, nominal wages may remain unchanged and real wages therefore rise.[2]

For Ricardo, then, two opposing tendencies are at work: the tendency of decreasing returns from land, which causes all prices to rise — not only those of agricultural and mining products but also those of industrial products because the latter contain raw materials of agricultural or mining origin;[3] and the tendency of falling prices, which results from the introduction of machines and other technical improvements. The first tendency is related to population growth and implies constant technology; the second implies technical change, that is, changes in the production functions. Ricardo recognized that, logically, the first tendency may be counterbalanced or more than counterbalanced by a reduction in protective tariffs on agricultural products and by the introduction of technical improvements in agriculture. But he was pessimistic about the chances of such compensation in practice. (In its absence, the process of accumulation comes to a halt, in Ricardo's view; agricultural prices rise and so do wages; the consequent fall in profits impairs the incentive and curtails the funds for accumulation.)

Smith's views do not contradict Ricardo's. Smith made a distinction between agricultural and industrial production from the point of view of the possibilities of further division of labor.[4]

---

[1] *Principles* (Sraffa edition), pp. 94–5.

[2] *Ibid.*, p. 392. See also below, Chapter 7.

[3] *Ibid.*, pp. 93, 117; *Essay on Profits* (Sraffa edition), IV, 20.

[4] J. A. Schumpeter, *History of Economic Analysis* (London, 1954), p. 259.

These possibilities, which in practice take the form of technical progress, are greater in industry than in agriculture, and hence the prices of industrial products must diminish not only absolutely but also relatively to those of agricultural products.[5]

So the mechanism which, according to the classical theorists, distributes the fruits of technical progress consists essentially of a long-term trend of falling prices and constant nominal incomes. This mechanism implies competition, or, as they would perhaps have said, this mechanism *is* competition.

Under monopoly the reduction in cost may have no effect at all on price, unless the monopolist who introduces technical improvements finds it profitable to alter the volume of output. The extent of any possible price reduction depends on the elasticity of demand. Under oligopoly, as we have seen, price reductions follow only from those cost reductions that are due to innovations accessible to firms of all sizes or to a fall in variable factor prices. Cost reductions due to new methods which, because of technological discontinuities, are not within reach of all firms lead not to price reductions but to increased profits. On the other hand, trade-union pressure or government intervention may cause cost reductions to be translated into higher wages.

In short, under monopoly and oligopoly the fruits of technical progress are only in part translated into price reductions (and as far as that part is concerned, one might say that under oligopoly a special type of competition is at work); in part, and increasingly so with greater concentration, they lead to higher nominal incomes.

There can be no doubt that at the time of the classical economists the mechanism they described was at work over wide areas. Since then the "oligopolistic (or monopolistic) mechanism" has gradually gained ground. Nevertheless, it is not so long ago that very distinguished economists were still basing their analysis on the assumption that the mechanism of competition was working, or at least could provide a useful reference base for the study of business cycles. Thus Schumpeter, when describing the essential

[5] *Wealth of Nations*, Book I, chap. 11, "Effects of the Progress of Improvement upon the Real Price of Manufactures."

elements of his theoretical model in his monumental *Business Cycles,* published in 1939, writes:

that sequence of phenomena [making up the business cycle] leads up to a new neighborhood of equilibrium, in which enterprise will start again. This new neighborhood of equilibrium is characterized, as compared to the one that preceded it, by a "greater" social product of a different pattern, new production functions, equal sum of money incomes, a minimum (strictly zero) rate of interest, zero profits, zero loans, *a different system of prices and a lower level of prices, the fundamental expression of the fact that all the lasting achievements of the particular spurt of innovation have been handed over to consumers in the shape of increased real incomes.*[6]

Schumpeter later refined and qualified his model and, both in the same work and in others,[7] discussed in detail the question of price flexibility in noncompetitive conditions; but, notwithstanding certain doubts and reservations,[8] he maintained that his concept, worked out some thirty years earlier, remained in substance realistic in the new situation.[9]

Comparison of the two mechanisms

The "oligopolistic (or monopolistic) mechanism," then, ultimately leads to relative price rigidity. To define this concept of rigidity more precisely, we have to refer back to the classical mechanism of competition.

As long as the mechanism of competition works, prices in the long run must diminish approximately in proportion to the increase in the productivity of labor (this is a first approximation; in a second approximation one would have to consider the differences in the relative amount of fixed capital entering into the production of different goods).[10] If, over time, prices fail to dimin-

---

[6] *Business Cycles,* I, 137. (My italics.)

[7] Vol. II, chap. 10, D, "Entrepreneurial Price Policies"; *Capitalism, Socialism, and Democracy,* chap. 8, "Monopolistic Practices."

[8] For example, *Business Cycles,* I, 144.

[9] See P. Sylos-Labini, "Il problema dello sviluppo economico in Marx ed in Schumpeter," *Teoria e politica dello sviluppo economico,* ed. G. U. Papi (Milan, 1954), pp. 103–4.

[10] See Robinson, *The Accumulation of Capital,* Book VII, chap. 34, "Normal Prices."

ish in that proportion, they are to be regarded as rigid, and the more so the larger is the discrepancy between changes in labor productivity and changes in price.[11]

If the fruits of technical progress can be spread either through falling prices or through rising money incomes, how do the results of the two methods compare?

Unless we try to find an answer to this question, it is quite impossible to work out an adequate theory of market forms. The static analysis of market forms cannot be other than superficial. For example, the proposition that monopoly tends to restrict production is commonly demonstrated with the help of static demand and supply curves, but it is open to unanswerable objections.[12] This question is one of fundamental importance, and it is hard to think of an economist who did not have to face it at some point or other in his work.

Nevertheless, there is an astonishing dearth of analysis of the consequences of the two methods. Such analyses as we possess are usually governed by immediate policy considerations rather than by theoretical ones; even where the theoretical purpose is foremost, it most often concerns the consequences for the distribution of national income rather than for its growth and for the level of employment. We are primarily interested in the latter group of consequences, but before discussing them it may be useful to take a brief look at some special aspects of the former.

Privileged firms

It has been said sometimes that monopolistic and oligopolistic formations tend to modify the distribution of the fruits of tech-

---

[11] In the present situation of almost chronic inflationary pressure, such a concept of long-run rigidity may appear absurd, or at best unrealistic. But we should not forget that throughout the nineteenth century the basic trend was for *all* prices to fall, and that the prices of industrial products definitely fell more than agricultural prices, just as the classical theory said they should. In England, the relatively moderate rise of real wages during the first half of the last century was principally due to a long-run price fall; in the second half of the century it came partly from rising nominal wages, but in large part also from falling prices. See J. H. Clapham, *An Economic History of Modern England*, I, *The Early Railway Age*, pp. 128, 561; W. T. Layton and G. Crowther, *An Introduction to the Study of Prices* (London, 1935).

[12] Schumpeter, *Capitalism, Socialism, and Democracy*, chaps. 7 and 8.

nical progress in the direction of greater inequality of incomes to the benefit of capitalistic and the detriment of labor incomes.[13] The argument is that price rigidity leads to growing profits. As we have seen, this apparently obvious observation is only partly true. In concentrated oligopoly, cost reductions may also lead to higher wages. The observation might apply only to the case of pure monopoly. We are thus led to consider the problem in more specific terms.

First of all, the oligopolistic mechanism leads to the emergence of privileged firms within industries. Some firms are able to obtain durably above-normal profits and, in the case of not generally accessible innovations and technical improvements, even growing profits. Moreover, the wage increases which large oligopolistic firms may concede under the pressure of trade-union action or in their own interests tend to throw the small and medium firms in the same industry into a permanent state of crisis. These firms must try to survive by opposing wage increases for their workers.

However, considering that there are imperfections in the labor market even within the separate industries, it is quite possible for the wages paid by firms of different size to differ considerably and durably. (The differences may reside not so much in actual wage rates as in other kinds of remuneration, such as productivity bonuses.) In this sense the larger firms become privileged both as regards profits and wages. The forces which tend to level out profits and wages do not become inoperative, but they encounter more friction and, sometimes, real obstacles.

Privileged industries

The oligopolistic, and even more so the monopolistic, mechanism may end up by creating whole privileged branches of production. If we consider the incomes (profits and wages) accruing to those who belong to a certain oligopolistic (or monopolistic) industry or set of industries, these incomes may durably and considerably exceed those of other industries, where market forms closer to competition prevail.

[13] See D. Lynch, *The Concentration of Economic Power* (New York, 1946), chap. 9, esp. p. 253.

The most conspicuous divergence is that which exists in many countries between "industry" and "agriculture." In industry the oligopolistic mechanism prevails, in agriculture the mechanism of competition, although the latter no longer operates in quite the same way as it would if it governed the entire economic system. In other words, in industry the prevailing tendency is for the fruits of technical progress to be distributed through rising money incomes rather than through falling prices; in agriculture the prevailing tendency is for prices to fall. The two tendencies do not operate in isolation; they meet or, better, clash because the two sectors are interrelated. They exchange producer and consumer goods. The oligopolistic mechanism causes the terms of trade in the exchange between industrial and agricultural products to move against agriculture, where competition prevails. Farmers purchase from industry consumer goods and, what is more important, producer goods at prices which are relatively, and sometimes absolutely, rising; they sell to industry raw materials and consumer goods at relatively falling prices. The exchange ratio between agricultural and industrial prices thus tends to deteriorate for agriculture, and this is precisely the opposite of what would happen under the classical mechanism and what in fact did happen during the whole of the nineteenth century.[14] This deterioration widens the gap between agricultural

[14] In the United States this exchange ratio has been called the "parity ratio" with reference to a given historical period. As is well known, this ratio has tended to worsen for American agriculture during the last thirty or forty years, despite the fact that output per man rose no more quickly — and indeed, until about twenty years ago, less quickly — in agriculture than in industry, and despite all the government's measures in support of farm prices. Farm price supports are, in substance, an attempt by the government to give agriculture a vicarious market power or, in other words, to give farmers *artificially* a counterweight to the market power which industry has been acquiring *spontaneously* by means of progressive concentration. In agriculture, as we have seen earlier (Introduction, n. 18), the process of concentration has not gone very far. But farm price supports, whatever their immediate results, have certainly led to a number of very serious difficulties. See P. Sylos-Labini, "Relative Prices and Development Programmes," *Banca del Lavoro Quarterly Review*, September 1957.

A similar deterioration has taken place in the prices of many important raw materials in relation to manufacturing prices, to the detriment of the countries specializing in the production of these raw materials. (See United Nations, *The Economic Development of Latin America*, Lake Success, 1950, II; H. W.

and industrial incomes, or impedes its diminution and perpetuates
it.

But here we have to add a few qualifications. First of all, the
agricultural prices under discussion are those which the producer
gets. If farmers can organize the marketing or industrial process-
ing of farm products, they can do much to reduce the relative
worsening of their position. (In both these activities noncompetitive market forms are the rule.)

Second, there is a distinction between "poor" agricultural
products, such as cereals, demand for which does not rise with
growing income or rises less than proportionately, and "rich"
products, such as livestock products and many fruits and vege-
tables, demand for which rises proportionately or more than
proportionately with income. (The income elasticity of demand is,
respectively, either lower or else equal to or higher than unity.)
If left to themselves, the relative prices of the poor products
certainly do tend to deteriorate systematically. But in the case
of rich products, growing income may even improve relative
prices. For this reason there is a growing tendency to switch
from poor crops to rich ones. If the changeover happens quickly
and the increasing supply keeps step with increasing demand
or even exceeds it, the relative prices of the rich products will
soon fall back to their previous levels or below. Everything depends on the presence of suitable land and on the speed of agricultural transformation — the quicker it is, the more short-lived
is the increase in relative prices. All in all, however, the transition from poor to rich farm produce may mitigate or sometimes
even offset the relative deterioration in the position of agriculture
as a whole.

Finally, there is the question of the natural and technical
conditions of agricultural production, which prevent it from ad-

Singer, "The Distribution of Gains between Investing and Borrowing Countries," *American Economic Review,* May 1950, pp. 473–85.) This obviously has
its bearing on the problems of underdeveloped countries and, in particular, on
the problem of the gap between them and the advanced countries, which tends
to grow as long as things are left to spontaneous economic forces.

If the considerations here advanced are correct, the relative fall in raw-materials prices, by which Kalecki in part explains the constancy of the share of
wages in national income, is not, as he thinks, "accidental" (see p. 87), but
is due to an organic process which has its origin in industrial concentration.

justing to market changes as readily as industrial output can do. In general, the relations between agriculture and industry have been examined precisely from this particular viewpoint, but a comprehensive analysis should extend to all aspects of the question, technical and economic alike. In the last resort, the inability of large-scale government intervention to stop the growing divergence between agricultural and industrial incomes is due to the different effects of the competitive and the oligopolistic mechanism.

In this context it may be interesting to recall what B. D. Giles has to say:

Industries are envisaged as lying along a scale of degrees of monopoly. At one end is agriculture, perfectly competitive; at the other end are the highly monopolized industries, such as iron and steel. The monopolized industries through their price and output policy restrict their own employment of factors, and their labour force also tends to be highly organized into trade unions in order to exploit a monopolistic position. Thus the supply of factors of production seeking employment in the competitive sectors of the economy is increased, and their price reduced, without a corresponding reduction in the price of factors which succeed in finding a place in the monopolized sectors. The competitive sectors of the economy become a refuge for units or resources excluded from employment elsewhere; of these competitive sectors agriculture is one of the largest, and of the resources affected labour is probably the most important.[15]

I am not inclined to agree with all of this (especially concerning "restriction of employment," which, in this formulation, is reminiscent of the static analysis of monopoly), but I would subscribe to the central thesis, which is in harmony with what is written above.

These brief observations about "privileged" firms and industries should be enough to show that the first aspect of the question, that of the two mechanisms' different consequences for the distribution of national income (among individuals, firms, and production sectors), cannot be separated from the other aspect of the question, that of the consequences for the level of national income and employment. We now turn to this second aspect.

[15] "Agriculture and the Price Mechanism," *Oxford Studies in the Price Mechanism*, p. 196.

VII

Introduction of Machinery, Growth of Income, and Level of Employment

The different consequences of the two mechanisms by which the fruits of technical progress are distributed can best be seen by going back to the classical problem of the introduction of new machines, which in effect is the main form of technical progress. The surest guide in such a difficult field is Ricardo himself and his famous discussion of the introduction of new machines (*Principles*, Chapter 31, "On Machinery").

Ricardo on the introduction of machinery

Ricardo's argument is so condensed that the best thing to do is to quote the relevant passages in full.[1] We shall single out three points: (1) the creation of unemployment as a result of the introduction of a new machine; (2) price reduction as a result of cost reduction, new capital formation, and subsequent increase in the demand for labor; (3) increase in real incomes (profits, rents, and wages) as a result of price reduction.

[1] A capitalist we will suppose employs a capital of the value of 20,000*l*. and that he carries on the joint business of a farmer, and a manufacturer of necessaries. We will further suppose, that 7000*l*. of this capital is invested in fixed capital, viz. in buildings, implements, etc. etc. and that the remaining 13,000*l*. is employed as circulating capital in the support of labour. Let us suppose, too, that profits are 10 per cent., and consequently that the capitalist's capital is every year put into its original state of efficiency, and yields a profit of 2000*l*.

---

[1] The page numbers in the text refer to Vol. I of the Sraffa edition.

Each year the capitalist begins his operations, by having food and necessaries in his possession of the value of 13,000*l.*, all of which he sells in the course of the year to his own workmen for that sum of money, and, during the same period, he pays them the like amount of money for wages: at the end of the year they replace in his possession food and necessaries of the value of 15,000*l.*, 2000*l.* of which he consumes himself, or disposes of as may best suit his pleasure and gratification. As far as these products are concerned, the gross produce for that year is 15,000*l.*, and the net produce 2000*l.* Suppose now, that the following year the capitalist employs half his men in constructing a machine, and the other half in producing food and necessaries as usual. During that year he would pay the sum of 13,000*l.* in wages as usual, and would sell food and necessaries to the same amount to his workmen; but what would be the case the following year?

While the machine was being made, only one-half of the usual quantity of food and necessaries would be obtained, and they would be only one-half the value of the quantity which was produced before. The machine would be worth 7500*l.*, and the food and necessaries 7500*l.*, and, therefore, the capital of the capitalist would be as great as before; for he would have besides these two values, his fixed capital worth 7000*l.*, making in the whole 20,000*l.* capital, and 2000*l.* profit. After deducting this latter sum for his own expenses, he would have a no greater circulating capital than 5500*l.* with which to carry on his subsequent operations; and, therefore, his means of employing labour would be reduced in the proportion of 13,000*l.* to 5500*l.*, and, consequently, all the labour which was before employed by 7500*l.* would become redundant (pp. 388–9).

[2] As, however, the power of saving from revenue to add to capital, must depend on the efficiency of the net revenue, to satisfy the wants of the capitalist, it could not fail to follow from the reduction in the price of commodities consequent on the introduction of machinery, that with the same wants he would have increased means of saving, — increased facility of transferring revenue into capital. But with every increase of capital he would employ more labourers; and, therefore, a portion of the people thrown out of work in the first instance, would be subsequently employed; and if the increased production, in consequence of the employment of the machine, was so great as to afford, in the shape of net produce, as great a quantity of food and necessaries as existed before in the form of gross produce, there would be the same ability to employ the whole population, and, therefore, there would not necessarily be any redundancy of people (p. 390).

[3] If the improved means of production, in consequence of the use of machinery, should increase the net produce of a country in a degree so great as not to diminish the gross produce, (I mean always quantity of commodities and not value,) then the situation of all classes will be improved. The landlord and capitalist will benefit, not by an increase of rent and profit, but by the advantages resulting from the expenditure of

the same rent, and profit, on commodities, very considerably reduced in value, while the situation of the labouring classes will also be considerably improved; 1st, from the increased demand for menial servants; 2dly, from the stimulus to savings from revenue, which such an abundant net produce will afford; and 3dly, from the low price of all articles of consumption on which their wages will be expended (p. 392).

Ricardo's main thesis (1) has been attacked more than once, but it is not easy to locate any serious criticism. The objection that the workers displaced by machines can later be reabsorbed by the firms which introduced the innovation, thanks to the decrease in prices and the expansion of demand, is beside the point. This is the first part of Ricardo's earlier thesis which he expressly repudiated in the chapter "On Machinery" that he added to the third edition of his *Principles*.[2] The second part of the thesis which Ricardo abandoned has also been raised as an objection to his new thesis, but his critics obviously did not bother to read the new chapter carefully. The second part of Ricardo's old thesis may be summarized as follows.

Even supposing that the increase in demand following upon a price reduction is not enough to enable all the unemployed to be absorbed again, another fact has to be taken into account. In Ricardo's own words (in the past tense because the passage refers to a time when the author still held those views):

as the capital which employed [the workers since replaced by machines] was still in being, and as it was the interest of those who had it to employ it productively, it appeared to me that it would be employed on the production of some other commodity, useful to the society, for which there could not fail to be a demand (p. 387).

The central point of Ricardo's new thesis is this: the introduction of machines causes some part of the circulating capital used for wage payments to be transformed into fixed capital. Contrary to the conclusions to which he was led by his old thesis, Ricardo now concludes that the formation of additional circulating capital is a necessary condition for the absorption of the unemployed; such additional capital is generated, according to Ricardo, by the decrease in prices.

[2] Pp. 386–8.

Wicksell's critique

Serious criticism has been leveled against Ricardo by Marx and Wicksell. Marx accepts the general doctrine but violently opposes certain specific points.[3] (These points, while important in themselves, have no particular relevance to the problem at hand and will be neglected.) Wicksell rejects the main argument, namely, that the introduction of machines generates unemployment.[4] Consider for a moment one point of Wicksell's argument, which epitomizes what we might call the neoclassical theory of incompatibility between unemployment and flexible wages.

Wicksell considers "an economic society which, from its natural circumstances, only produces one or a few staple articles — and which must consequently procure all other commodities from other places or countries at exchange values which are determined in the world market, independently of anything they may do." [5] Because of this special assumption, the prices of all products are given and remain constant throughout the whole process under examination. For the sake of simplicity, Wicksell also assumes an initial situation with only two factors of production, land and labor, and abstracts from capital. He then introduces into his system new machines which render a certain number of workers "superfluous." So far Wicksell is in agreement with Ricardo. But he is then led to conclude, unlike Ricardo, that total gross product cannot diminish but must increase, and that the workers rendered superfluous by the introduction of the machines will necessarily be reabsorbed. Here is what Wicksell says:

Let us assume that the introduction of labour-saving agricultural machinery (haymaking machines, horse-harrows, etc.) has made a predominantly pastoral agriculture more profitable, other things being equal, than arable farming; so that the value of the product, though certainly less, produces a larger net yield, owing to the saving of labour. The direct consequence must then be that one or more farmers will go over to the more profitable form of production. If all were to follow their example, there would

[3] *Theorien über den Mehrwert* (Dietz, Stuttgart, 1905): II, *David Ricardo*, chap. 4.
[4] *Lectures*, I, 133–44.
[5] *Ibid.*, p. 136.

certainly be a more or less considerable diminution of the total product (or of its exchange value), *but this does not happen*. For as soon as a number of labourers have been made superfluous by these changes, and wages have accordingly fallen, then, as Ricardo failed to see, the old methods of production — in this case the old arable farming — will become more profitable; they will develop, using labour more intensively, and absorb the surplus of idle labourers. It can be rigorously proved that equilibrium in this case necessarily presupposes a *division* of production between the old and the new methods so that the net profits of the entrepreneur will be equally great in both branches of production and the total product, or its exchange value, will reach the maximum physically possible, and will thus finally increase, and not decrease (pp. 137–8).

This argument is logically unexceptionable, granted Wicksell's assumptions. But his assumptions are different from Ricardo's, and it is strange that Wicksell should not have noticed this.[6]

First of all, Wicksell introduces the machines from outside (they are presumably imported from abroad); if he had assumed them to be produced domestically, he would have had to examine the effects of the wage reductions on production cost and on the price of the machines themselves. He could not have broken off his analysis where he did: with lower wages, the machines would cost less and, on his own assumptions, the substitution of machines for workers would continue.

But the fundamental differences between Wicksell's and Ricardo's assumptions are those which concern wages and prices. Wicksell's argument presupposes flexible wages and rigid prices; Ricardo, on the other hand, implicitly but quite unmistakeably assumes (as he always does) that wages are rigid downward, and he explicitly assumes that prices are flexible. With the assumption of rigid prices Wicksell changes the terms in which Ricardo poses the problem, and he excludes from the outset precisely what Ricardo regards as the fundamental condition of the *later* possible reabsorption of the workers rendered superfluous at the beginning.

Even more significant is the difference between the assumptions concerning wages. Ricardo assumes wages to be rigid downward; Wicksell assumes them to be flexible. At the end of his argument, Wicksell feels a doubt and asks himself whether his

[6] Wicksell accuses Ricardo of having stopped halfway: "Ricardo has here failed to draw the final conclusions from his own assumptions" (p. 137).

results would be upset if it were assumed that wages are at the subsistence level and therefore not further compressible. He considers that the result would still be valid because in his view it is perfectly reasonable to consider even such wages flexible, insofar as the workers can draw upon relief: in that case subsistence wages can fall and remain indefinitely below the subsistence level.[7]

Now it is just here that the limits as well as the congenital weakness of Wicksell's argument become evident. All he does is to compare three equilibrium positions: the initial one, the one following immediately upon the introduction of machines, and the final equilibrium when the workers have been reabsorbed because of a fall in wages. But if we assume mechanization of production to be an uninterrupted process, we would arrive at the absurd conclusion that unemployment can gradually be absorbed only by progressive wage decreases. Wages, in other words, would have to tend toward zero.[8] The process would be arrested long before that point because of the progressive contraction of demand; but then the continuance of mechanization is logically incompatible with wages that have perfect downward flexibility. (Note that Wicksell, like Ricardo, starts out with the assumption that the machines are introduced not after a rise in wages,[9] but autonomously and independently of any change in wages.)

Thus Ricardo's assumption of wage rigidity is fully justified. Indeed, the kind of reasoning Ricardo applies is much more appropriate to the problem at hand. Unlike Wicksell, Ricardo does not worry about final equilibrium, but examines first the forces which expel the workers from the productive process and then the forces which cause them to be reabsorbed. On the first point his analysis is thorough; on the second, he merely gives general indications — the process of absorption of labor is set in motion by the formation of additional capital, which in turn depends on the price decrease.

But what happens if we assume not only wages but also prices

---

[7] *Lectures*, I, 141.

[8] The workers would become an army on the dole — on the dole as a result of technical progress!

[9] Ricardo discusses this hypothesis, as distinct from the one treated in the text, in the first chapter of his *Principles*.

to be rigid downward? This is what interests us most here. To find the answer, we must compare the effects on income and employment of the classical mechanism, on the one hand, with those of the oligopolistic mechanism, on the other. We shall not concern ourselves with the final equilibrium, nor, for the time being, shall we raise the problem of "equilibrium unemployment" (as we shall see presently, this problem is not necessarily of a static nature). Rather, we shall try to examine the manner of operation of the two sets of forces, those which reduce and those which raise employment, by supposing all conditions to remain equal except for price rigidity.

A three-sector model

To compare the effects of the two mechanisms, we shall have to work out a theoretical model. It is obvious that it would be quite unsatisfactory to employ a one-firm model. To use familiar language: we have to work out a "general equilibrium" rather than a "partial equilibrium" model.

On reflection, Ricardo's numerical example quoted above does not really concern a single "firm," but a closed system. In substance, it fulfills the requirements of a general equilibrium model. Ricardo makes the extremely simplifying assumption that one and the same "capitalist" produces consumer goods and, at a certain point, capital goods (machines). Thus, Ricardo considers together the two production sectors of the social economy which Marx considers separately.

However, Ricardo's model does not enable us to make the comparison which interests us here. Moreover, if we assume that prices do not diminish after the introduction of the machines, two extreme cases are possible: (1) the difference between prices and lower costs is durably translated into higher profits; (2) this difference is translated into higher wages, which go entirely to consumption.[10] Case 1 divides into three extreme subcases: the higher profits go (a) entirely to consumption, (b) entirely to investment, or (c) entirely to hoarding. The analytical difficulties

---

[10] It would be more realistic to assume that wage earners have a lower propensity to save than capitalists, but not a zero propensity. However, this assumption would needlessly complicate the subsequent argument without altering its substance.

involved in working out a model to take account of all these different possibilities are obviously very great.

A model of the type proposed by Leontief may be of help; for our purposes, the bare essentials are enough. Two sectors (producer and consumer goods) are not enough; we need at least two sectors of producer goods in order to analyze the reciprocal consequences of cost reductions due to variations in the price of producer goods of a given type. We need three sectors: (I) machine sector; (II) raw-materials sector; (III) consumer-goods sector.

The first and second sector each produces for its own use as well as for the use of the other two sectors. The equilibrium conditions for the whole system are as follows: the money value of the machines employed in the three sectors must equal the value of the first sector's output; the money value of the raw materials used in the three sectors must equal the value of the second sector's output; the sum of wages and profits must equal the value of the output of the third sector (assuming that both wages and profits go entirely to consumption and the economy thus is stationary). A numerical example fulfilling these conditions is set out in tabulation below.

	I Machines	II Raw materials	III Consumer goods	Value of sales
Machines	1000	1000	1000	3000
Raw materials	1000	1000	1000	3000
Wages	700	700	700⎫	3000
Profits	300	300	300⎭	
Value of purchases	3000	3000	3000	

The first sector sells to each of the three sectors machines of a money value of 1000, so that its sales receipts are 3000 (300 machines at a price of 10 each). Similarly, the second sector sells raw materials worth 3000. The third sector sells consumer goods worth 2100 to wage earners and worth another 900 to entrepreneurs; altogether it sells consumer goods of a value of 3000. The stationary system is in equilibrium. Suppose that each worker's wage is equal to one money unit; total employment is therefore 2100. The profit rate is equal to 10 percent of the value of total sales, or 11.1 percent (one ninth) of the total money cost. (We always refer the profit rate to the value of annual sales or to total annual cost; strictly speaking, it should be referred to the entire capital invested. But this would complicate the argument unnecessarily.) The model represents *flows* during a given period, say one year. Therefore, if we suppose that each machine has a lifetime of ten years, an annual output of 300 machines implies that 3000 machines are in operation at any one time.

Suppose now — to follow the argument more easily, refer to the table opposite — that the firms which produce raw materials learn that the firms in the first sector are in a position to construct new types of machines, which will make it possible to mechanize certain production processes and so to effect an annual saving in the wage bill greater than the annual cost of the new machines. (For simplicity, we shall assume this cost to consist only of amortization and maintenance charges.) In these circumstances, the raw-materials firms decide not to distribute any profits for the year, and they use the 300 money units so saved to order 30 of these new machines (which have the same price as the existing ones).

To produce the 30 new machines, the first sector needs to employ 70 additional workers, 10 additional machines, and 10 additional units of raw materials. In the initial situation there was full employment; during the transition period there is a break in the consumption of the profits of the second sector. Therefore, the additional factors of production needed in the first sector are withdrawn from the third; the output of the third sector contracts correspondingly. (We assume constant returns to scale.)

In the period during which the new machines are introduced, the situation is as shown in column 2 of the table. There is as yet no unemployment, but the distribution of the workers among the three sectors has changed.

In the following period, when the new machines enter into operation and the additional demand for machines contracts, the demand for machines is determined only by the gradual replacement and repair of worn-out machines, old and new. Supposing that every machine has a lifetime of ten years, the second sector's

		New equilibrium (constant prices)	
			Case 1(a)	Case 2
Sector	Initial situation	Transition period[a]	Higher profits (consumed)	Higher wages
	1	2	3	4
I. Machines				
Wages	700	770	707	707
Machines	1000	1100	1010	1010
Raw materials	1000	1100	1010	1010
	2700	2970	2727	2727
Profits	300	330	303	303
	3000	3300	3030	3030
II. Raw materials				
Wages	700	700	400	670
Machines	1000	1300	1030	1030
Raw materials	1000	1000	1000	1000
	2700	3000	2430	2700
Profits	300	—	570	300
	3000	3000	3000	3000
III. Consumer goods				
Wages	700	630	693	693
Machines	1000	900	990	990
Raw materials	1000	900	990	990
	2700	2430	2673	2673
Profits	300	270	297	297
	3000	2700	2970	2970
Employment	2100	2100	1800	1800
Unemployment	—	—	300	300
Total profits	900	900	1170	900
Total wages	2100	1800	1800	2070
Wage per worker (in money units)	1	1	1	$\begin{cases} 1^b \\ 1.675^c \end{cases}$
Unit price of machines	10	10	10	10
Unit price of raw materials	10	10	10	10
Unit price of consumer goods	10	10	10	10
Output of consumer goods in physical units (consumable income)	300	270	297	297

[a] New machines introduced in Sector II. [b] Sectors I and III. [c] Sector II.

demand for machines and spare parts has durably increased by an amount equal to one tenth of the value of the additional machines.[11] But, once the new machines are in operation, 300 workers are dismissed from the second sector. Total employment falls from 2100 to 1800 workers. The total costs of the second sector fall, and its profits rise from 300 to 570.

If we compare the new equilibrium situation with the initial situation, we see that, owing to the second sector's increased demand for machines and spare parts destined to replace and repair worn-out machines, the first sector has somewhat expanded its output at the expense of the third sector. If, now, the higher profits of the second sector are entirely spent on consumer goods, the output of the third sector expands above what it was in the transition period but does not quite reach its initial level (column 3). At this point we must look more specifically at the different possible cases.

Alternative consequences of a cost reduction

Cost reduction may have three possible consequences: (1) higher profits, which are either (a) consumed, (b) invested, that is, spent on the purchase of factors of production, or (c) hoarded; (2) higher wages, which are consumed; (3) lower prices — insofar as the price fall affects producer goods, firms have lower costs and expand investment.[12]

We assume constant prices for cases 1 and 2. In cases 1(a) and 1(b) the second sector durably obtains above-normal profits (23.4 percent instead of 11.1 percent) because of the existence of oligopolistic or monopolistic formations. In case 2 the workers of the second sector earn higher money wages than the workers in the other two sectors (1.675 compared with 1); the differential

[11] In the transition from the initial situation to the period of introduction of the new machines, and then from the latter situation to the period when the machines are functioning, a process takes place which resembles the "accelerator." However, it is resemblance rather than equality: the accelerator is set in motion by variations in the rate of change of demand for consumer goods, while the process here examined is set in motion by a change in technical data.

[12] The term "investment" is here used in a broad sense, covering not only fixed capital but all factors of production.

is perpetuated by the "natural," as well as the oligopolistic and monopolistic, obstacles to the mobility of labor.

Consumption and employment are equal in cases 1(a) and 2. Whether the cost reduction is translated into higher profits entirely consumed, or into higher wages, total income is the same and the unemployment created by the introduction of the new machines in the second sector is not absorbed. If the additional profits are not consumed or invested, but are hoarded and disappear from circulation, equilibrium is disrupted: prices fall, the output of consumer goods falls, unemployment rises, and profits diminish. In substance, this is Keynes's "banana case." [13] Of course, the subcases of additional profit can be combined in various ways; the profit increment may be partly consumed, partly invested, and partly hoarded.

Case 1(c) is one of disequilibrium. In cases 1(a) and 2 — consumption of the profit increment or of the wage increment in the second sector — the introduction of the new machines will be followed by stationary conditions, with constant national income and employment.

By contrast, progress is possible in cases 1(b) — investment of the profit increment, at constant prices — and 3 — lower prices, permitting larger saving and investment. As in case 2, we assume that in case 3, too, the workers save nothing; the firms save more as a result of the lower prices of producer goods.

Let us look more closely into case 1(b). With total costs of 2430, normal profits in the second sector would be 270 (one ninth of 2430); in actual fact, profits are 570, so the profit increment is 300 money units. By hypothesis, this profit increment is invested. What is the distribution of the new investment? Obviously, the firms of the second sector which make the additional profits cannot invest them all in the same sector without creating intersectoral imbalance. Balanced development is possible only on the assumption that the new investment gradually spreads throughout all the sectors in the proportions shown in column 3; these proportions reflect the technical coefficients in the three sectors after the introduction of the new machines.

[13] *Treatise on Money*, I, 176–8.

Once the additional profits have been invested, total production and employment rise. The unemployed workers are absorbed at least in part, and total profits rise further. There is no reason why we should not imagine that such a development might continue, through successive investment of each further profit increment, until the limit of full employment is reached.

But can this really happen in the world as it is, without shocks and interruptions? We shall see later (especially in Chapter 10) that the main obstacles to complete reinvestment of profits come from the demand side. But there are difficulties also from the sole point of view of the formation and distribution of investable funds. The important point to remember is that the additional saving, which becomes disposable for investment, occurs in the firms of only one of the three sectors — in the firms of the raw-materials sector which have introduced the new machines. If development is to proceed in a balanced and uninterrupted fashion, these firms must invest part of their additional profits in the other sectors in just the right proportion. Now, each firm no doubt is fairly familiar with the conditions of its own market and so invests its savings internally without much delay; but when it comes to investing in other markets, firms meet with serious difficulties because of greater uncertainty and risk both for the lender and the borrower. The banking system and the stock exchange are of only limited help in overcoming these difficulties, because of what Kalecki has called "the principle of increasing risk." [14] As far as our problem is concerned, this can be expressed by saying that the firms' propensity to invest their own funds in their own business — by self-financing — is greater than their propensity to invest borrowed funds. More than that, the ability to obtain loans is not evenly distributed among firms. The greatest difficulties are encountered in obtaining long-term loans for the purpose of acquiring machines and other durable capital goods; only large and very large firms can borrow easily on such terms.

This sort of difficulty does not arise in case 3. Costs diminish not only for technical but also for economic reasons. The first

[14] *Essays in the Theory of Economic Fluctuations* (London, 1938), pp. 95–106.

to diminish are the technical coefficients of the firms which introduce the new machines; later, costs fall generally, as an accompaniment to the reduction in the prices of the goods employed as factors of production in various firms. As a result, profits rise above normal and firms find themselves in a position to effect additional investments. The process gradually spreads to all firms, large and small, in all sectors. The development does not depend upon external finance; outside loans may be contracted, but they are not a necessary condition of the process of development.[15]

The process is in substance the same as that described by the classical economists. New machines are introduced. For a certain time the firms introducing them enjoy extraordinary profits; but, with the spreading of the new machines to other firms, production increases and prices diminish. Insofar as the price fall affects

---

[15] Some aspects of the process which takes place gradually as costs and prices diminish can be illustrated by means of our numerical example. At first, costs diminish in the raw-materials sector, because of the decrease in the technical coefficients. Since in this case, 3, prices are by assumption flexible, raw-materials prices tend to fall gradually as costs fall. But raw materials are employed also in the first sector, which produces machines. Lower raw-materials prices lead to lower machine prices *and hence* to lower costs in the raw-materials sector *and hence* to lower costs in the machine sector, and so on. To find the new equilibrium prices all we need do is to solve a system of two equations, since the goods produced by the third sector do not enter into the other two sectors' costs — they are bought by the wage and profit earners of all three sectors. The technical coefficients to be used are those after the introduction of the machines (column 3). Since in this case there can be no above-normal profits, the profit rate in all three sectors is one ninth of the total cost. The system of equations is as follows (x is the price of the machines and y the price of raw materials):

$$707 + 101x + 101y + 1/9 \ (707 + 101x + 101y) = 303x,$$
$$400 + 103x + 100y + 1/9 \ (400 + 103x + 100y) = 300y.$$

The solution is

$$x = 8.55,$$
$$y = 7.53.$$

The price of consumer goods can now be easily found. All we need do is to replace the old by the new prices as the multipliers of the physical units of machines and raw materials employed in the third sector. The calculation yields a price of 8.55, the same as the price of machines.

Note that the cost reduction is greater in the sector where costs fall as a result of changes in the technical coefficients than in the sectors which benefit only from an indirect cost reduction, due to the process of diffusion which gradually lowers the prices of the factors of production. This accords with common sense and can be understood at once.

goods used as factors of production by firms in the other sectors, it means a cost reduction. The cost reduction calls forth a rise in profits above the normal level and the profit increment is invested. The process repeats itself and spreads. Production increases and profits return to normal.

This process, too, encounters frictions of various kinds, but not the particular difficulties inherent in case 1(b). These difficulties are not unsurmountable; growth of income and absorption of unemployment are possible in case 1(b) as well, but in practice the frictions are greater than in case 3. In particular, the process of absorption of unemployment is bound to be slower and more limited because it leaves out those medium and small firms which introduce no innovations and which can obtain long-term external financing only at much greater difficulty than the large firms.

In case 1(b) the processes of income growth and absorption of unemployment also come up against other obstacles which are either absent or at least much milder in case 3. To be profitable in case 1(b), the additional investments must be made *at the same time* in the various sectors, since only then can reciprocal outlets be created by way of an increase in the incomes of the suppliers of factors of production. In case 3, prices fall gradually and therefore the firms in the various sectors increase their investment gradually. Where investment expands first, there prices fall first, and the price fall does not ruin firms because their costs had decreased beforehand.

Interpretation of the analysis

Whenever prices remain constant and the cost reduction is translated into higher incomes, the growth of aggregate income and the absorption of unemployment either do not take place at all or happen more slowly and within narrower limits than when prices fall in proportion with costs.

More particularly, in cases 1(a) and 2 — consumption of the profit or wage increment — the introduction of new machines leads to a stationary situation: technological unemployment becomes permanent. In case 1(b) — constant prices and investment of the additional profits — aggregate income grows and unemployment can be completely absorbed. But the process encounters more serious difficulties than in case 3, where prices fall gradually with the cost reduction. In the latter case, the process tends to be not only faster but more widespread: it extends to all firms in all sectors.

Cases 1(a), 1(b), and 2 — as well as the special case 1(c) — are the consequence of what we have characterized as the oligopolistic or monopolistic mechanism of the distribution of the fruits of technical progress (constant prices, increase in money incomes); case 3 is peculiar to the competitive or classical mechanism (constant money incomes, falling prices).

As far as employment is concerned, the difference between the consequences of the two mechanisms resides in the fact that, while the forces tending to create unemployment are equally strong, those tending toward re-employment of labor are weaker and operate more slowly in the case of the oligopolistic mechanism.

As far as growth of income is concerned, the reasons for the greater merit of the classical mechanism are obvious. The diminution of prices concerns not only, and not so much, the consumers alone; insofar as goods more or less widely employed as factors of production become cheaper, the beneficiaries are the producers. In the final analysis, it is again the consumers who are favored by this process, and, indeed, their ultimate gain is considerably greater than any immediate increase in their money incomes that might have taken place instead. The reduction in the prices of producer goods has an influence on the costs, and hence on the prices, and hence again on the costs of innumerable other goods; the diffusion of the successive cost reductions eventually affects all firms, whatever their size, and is much wider than in any other case.

If, on the other hand, prices do not fall and money incomes rise gradually as changes in the technical coefficients cause the productivity of labor to increase, then the process of diffusion either does not take place at all or comes up against greater obstacles: the fruits of technical progress accrue primarily to the income recipients in the sector where progress originated, and, at that, the fruits are less abundant than those reaped from the process of diffusion.

Some economists maintain that as long as the productivity of labor rises, it is, or can be, a matter of indifference whether the increase is translated into higher wages or lower prices.[16] The preceding analysis invalidates this view, which, however, may be justified with other assumptions and other arguments. Thus it is possible to maintain that, given the prevalence of oligopolistic and monopolistic formations, prices would not fall in any case. A wage increase then seems a smaller evil than an increase in profits because in practice the workers' propensity to consume is much higher than the entrepreneurs': when wages rise, the danger of disequilibrium discussed above — case 1(c) — is less, and in the extreme case nonexistent, but it is high when profits rise. Only in terms of this alternative can it be said that an increase in money wages has positive effects on national income and employment. The fact remains that, in comparison with falling prices, the effect of rising nominal wages is negative insofar as it impedes (or, rather, circumscribes and hence greatly reduces) the diffusion of the fruits of technical progress.

We have compared extreme cases. On the one side, we have

[16] One exponent of this thesis is, for instance, Joan Robinson (*The Accumulation of Capital,* chap. 9, "Technical Progress," section on "Underconsumption"). In discussing the case where prices do not fall with costs because of the presence of monopolistic formations, she writes: "[In such a case] the main defence against the tendency to stagnation comes from pressure by trade unions to raise money-wage rates. When they succeed, the stickiness of prices tells in their favour, for entrepreneurs may prefer (within limits) to accept a cut in margins rather than to alter their price policy. In so far as this occurs, real-wage rates rise. If by this means real wages can be made to rise as fast as output per man the root of the trouble is cut, and the economy can accumulate capital and increase total product at the rate appropriate to the pace at which technical improvements are being introduced, *just as though competition were still active."* (My italics.)

Now it is true that Mrs. Robinson bases her thesis on very restrictive assumptions, including (1) that the consumption of profits is zero and (2) that technical progress is evenly distributed throughout the various branches of the economy. If these assumptions are granted, she is right, but the question is precisely whether they are admissible. When I raised doubts on this point in a letter to Mrs. Robinson, she replied: "The case of 'biased' progress with rentiers [in a broad sense, recipients of profits and other nonlabor incomes] in the model is certainly very complicated. I am not sure if I agree with your argument. If money wages rise in proportion to total productivity they rise less than in proportion to the sector which is progressing fastest [from the technical point of view], so that there is still some change in relative prices. This is a very tricky question to work out."

considered four cases of constant prices and increased money incomes and, on the other, the case of constant incomes and reduced prices. The first four cases correspond to the oligopolistic and monopolistic mechanism; the fifth, to the mechanism of competition.

In the real world, prices do not necessarily remain unchanged when costs are reduced, neither under monopoly nor under oligopoly.[17] In particular, under oligopoly prices will be reduced in proportion to cost whenever the initial cost reduction is general or is capable of becoming general (a fall in the price of variable factors or the introduction of technical innovations accessible to all firms). Nevertheless, the general model is valid. It remains true that under competition technical progress *tends* to be wholly translated into a price reduction, whereas under oligopoly it tends to be so translated only in part. Hence, under oligopoly, the consequences for income growth and for the level of employment tend to be closer to the cases of the first group.

Long-run price rigidity and economic policy

We can say, then, that the favorable effects of technical progress on income and employment are far more marked when the mechanism of competition is in operation than in any of the cases which can conceivably result from the oligopolistic mechanism. In this sense, the former mechanism is more advantageous to the economy as a whole.

However, caution is indicated in drawing conclusions for economic policy. One might be tempted, on the evidence of the comparison, to conclude that downward flexibility of prices is preferable to upward flexibility of money incomes and that it would be right, therefore, to pursue a policy of flexible prices. But then it should be remembered that the price flexibility which is a spontaneous feature of competition is structurally impossible in oligopoly, and particularly in concentrated oligopoly. The process of concentration of firms, with the technological discontinuities which it necessarily entails and gradually accentuates, generates an industrial structure which is congenitally incompatible with competition. If we suppose, for the sake of argument, that all

[17] See above, p. 105.

concerted action among oligopolistic entrepreneurs, such as is implied by the full-cost principle, can be abolished, the result would be not price flexibility but price chaos.[18] On the other hand, if one were to impose reductions in prices and wages, the results would obviously not be the same as those which come about spontaneously under competition. In other words, competition cannot be artificially restored. Nevertheless, it is reasonable to recommend policies designed to regulate prices and wages in some manner deemed fruitful for economic development and in the choice of which one may well draw on the lessons of the above comparison. Such prescriptions are reasonable insofar as they recognize the structural impossibility of certain spontaneous adjustments. Equally reasonable are legislation and government intervention designed to contain the market power of oligopolistic groups, or to modify its consequences. Measures aiming at reducing market power may be successful especially insofar as

[18] This has actually happened occasionally, especially during the first phase of the Great Depression, in the early 1930s. The American oil industry offers an example. When the depression coincided with the discovery of one of the world's largest and most abundant oilfields in Texas, the large oil companies lost practically all control over prices for a certain time. Prices became exceedingly mobile and tumbled to ludicrous levels, and losses and waste were enormous. Eventually, the proration system was introduced and its effect was to transform almost the entire American oil industry into a huge cartel. This system has been criticized by many American economists inasmuch as it creates, or consolidates, monopolistic power. The critics are only too right. But the alternative is not, and cannot be, a revival of competition, which is structurally impossible; the alternative is a change in the public regulations concerning that industry. See P. Sylos-Labini and G. Guarino, *L'industria petrolifera*, Part I, chap. 6.

From the theoretical point of view, we may recall some observations by Joseph A. Schumpeter and Oskar Lange.

Schumpeter, *Business Cycles*, II, 541: "If a cartel breaks down, or if a quasi-equilibrium among oligopolists is disturbed, it does not follow that we may now substitute the competitive schema to the one that applied before. On the contrary, there will be what we call a Disorganized Market."

Schumpeter, *Capitalism, Socialism, and Democracy*, p. 95: "under the conditions created by capitalist evolution, perfect and universal flexibility of prices might in depression further unstabilize the system, instead of stabilizing it as it no doubt would under the conditions envisaged by general theory."

Lange, *Price Flexibility and Employment*, Cowles Commission Monograph No. 8 (Bloomington, 1944), p. 87: "the mere removal of oligopolistic and oligopsonistic rules would result in general unpredictability of other firms' reactions, a state which may be fittingly described as 'oligopolistic (or oligopsonistic) chaos.' "

that market power derives from imperfections of the law, from tariff protection, or from other extraneous or "artificial" elements. But imperfect laws and, generally speaking, artificial elements do not, in modern economies, create but merely buttress oligopolistic market power, which has structural and ultimately technological origins. It would be an illusion, therefore, to place too much hope on policies of this variety.

We are led to conclude that our comparison between the two mechanisms has only limited value in providing policy foundations. The comparison is abstract in character and has analytical rather than practical value: it serves to bring out the different effects of the two mechanisms, as well as the difficulties which arise when the mechanism of competition comes more and more to be replaced by the mechanism of oligopoly and monopoly.

VIII

The Creation and Reabsorption of Technological Unemployment

A firm's annual total cost consists of (a) salaries and other overhead; (b) expenditures for durable producer goods; (c) inventory investment; (d) wages; and (e) expenditure for raw materials and other nondurable producer goods used up during the year. Demand for labor is influenced by (d) and in some part by (a); the cost elements (b) and (c) are investment expenditures in the strict sense.[1]

When the technical coefficients do not change, an increase in production is preceded by a proportional increase in all factors of production. When the coefficients change, production may expand by virtue of an increase in investment alone, without any increase in the demand for labor. Demand for labor may increase less than proportionately with output or, at the other extreme, it may fall while output expands. Generally, changes in the technical coefficients are due to a change in the type of investment goods, especially as regards durable producer goods, that is, plant and machinery. Only in the case of investment which does not occasion a change in the coefficients is it legitimate to assume, as modern economists often do, that the volume of investment and the level of employment vary proportionally.

But the other kind of investment, that associated with a change in technical coefficients, is of primary importance — so much so

---

[1] In classical theory, "capital" and "capital accumulation" encompass all the expenditures which firms make to acquire factors of production, including the services of labor; modern economists speak of "capital" and "capital formation," with reference either to the firm or to the whole of society, as the stock of real goods (buildings, plant, machines, inventories) employed in production and as the increase in that stock of goods through investment, in the strict sense of the word.

that it is the determining factor of economic development. Unless the technical coefficients change, economic development cannot go on indefinitely, if only because of the direct or indirect effects of the diminishing returns of land; the overall rate of increase in production would be bound to diminish and, in the long run, would tend toward zero.[2] Development can go on indefinitely only if technical coefficients change not merely occasionally but systematically, that is, as a result of a series of innovating investment. Such investment consists primarily of new and improved machines, which have the effect of lowering the labor coefficient and which, for this reason, may well generate technological unemployment.

It is generally recognized today that, in capitalistic economies, economic development and cyclical fluctuations are two aspects of one and the same process.[3] At the root of the process there is investment, which, depending on its nature and volume, generates two opposing forces: forces which attract labor and forces which repel labor. These forces vary in intensity over time: in the upward phase of the cycle the former are stronger (and unemployment tends to fall); in the downward phase the latter prevail (and unemployment tends to rise).

Keynes and the relationship between investment
and employment

The thesis of proportionality between variations in investment and employment was first propounded by Adam Smith,[4] then criticized by Ricardo, and eventually rehabilitated by Keynes in his *General Theory*.[5] This proposition is valid only on the as-

---

[2] Strangely enough, the fact that it is impossible for total production to rise indefinitely as long as the technical coefficients remain unchanged escaped the notice of the most distinguished theoretician of innovations (that is, of investment implying a change in coefficients). Schumpeter in fact speaks of "growth" at unchanged coefficients (as distinct from "development" originated by innovations) without mentioning any limits (*Business Cycles*, I, 83).

[3] See P. Sylos-Labini, "Il problema dello sviluppo economico in Marx ed in Schumpeter," pp. 72–5, 78–9, 95–6, 101–2.

[4] *Wealth of Nations*, Book I, chap. 9: "The demand for labour increases with the increase of stock, whatever be its profits." For Ricardo's critique, see "On Machinery," *Principles*.

[5] *The General Theory of Employment, Interest and Money* (London, 1936). Although the classical concept of "investment" (capital accumulation) is not

134   THE FRUITS OF TECHNICAL PROGRESS

sumption of unchanged technique and unchanged wages and machine prices.

Keynes did not make this proposition his own before the *General Theory*. In *Treatise on Money*⁶ he agreed with Schumpeter's thesis of fluctuations in fixed-capital investment, which thesis of course necessarily implies innovations. In an article written toward the end of 1930, Keynes expressed the opinion he held at that time⁷ as follows:

> The increase of technical efficiency has been taking place faster than we can deal with the problem of labour absorption; . . . the banking and monetary system of the world has been preventing the rate of interest from falling as fast as equilibrium requires.⁸

But Keynes was mainly concerned with the second problem, that of monetary and credit policy. He wanted to find out what part the banking system and discount policy were playing in accentuating or attenuating the fluctuations in investment and employment. In the *Treatise,* he had recognized not only the existence but the importance of the problem of technological change. However, he had done so only in general and formal terms, and there is some doubt whether the theoretical construction of the *Treatise* is always consistent with this recognition, since the assumption of constant technique is logically essential for several of his propositions. In the *General Theory,* Keynes decided to neglect technological change altogether and explicitly and consistently assumed constant technology. Keynes's theoretical con-

---

the same as Keynes's, the difference is irrelevant for the question under discussion here (see n. 1).

⁶ 1st ed. (1930), II, 95f.

⁷ Keynes referred specifically to the depression which had taken hold in the United States in 1929; but in Great Britain unemployment had been high and economic conditions relatively depressed ever since the end of the First World War.

⁸ The quotation is from an article originally published in *The Nation and Athenaeum,* October 11, 1930, and reprinted in J. M. Keynes, *Essays in Persuasion* (London, 1931), p. 358. Six pages later Keynes writes: "We are being afflicted with a new disease of which some readers may not yet have heard the name, but of which they will hear a great deal in the years to come — namely, technological unemployment." To call technological unemployment a "new disease" was perhaps exaggerated, even in an article for a popular magazine. However, its readers certainly heard a great deal about technological unemployment later, though not from Keynes.

struction may thereby have gained in logical rigor, but it lost in realism.

After the *General Theory*, then, Adam Smith's assumption of a direct relationship between investment and employment was again fashionable. As we have seen, this assumption is valid only in conditions of unchanged technique, that is, if we abstract from technical progress. But if Marx and Schumpeter are right, the capitalistic system is inconceivable without technical progress, or without continual technological change. In these circumstances we need in our analysis not only Smith's assumption but Ricardo's as well. The latter's reintroduction is all the more necessary in a period such as ours, when the rate of mechanization of the productive process is faster than ever before.[9]

Keynes's assumption of constant technical coefficients is generally held to be realistic for the short period because the construction of new plant and the introduction of new machines require a time span considerable enough to be described as a "long period." But the replacement of machines gradually wearing out affords *continual* opportunities for introducing quite important changes in the technical coefficients, if only because the producers of machines, on their own initiative, keep making better and better models. This kind of replacement is a gradual process which forms part of normal business management; the assumption of technological change, therefore, can logically be applied also to the short period.

We have the evidence of statistics and empirical studies, some of which we shall have occasion to quote, to prove that this process is, in practice, so important that it may not be neglected even by a first-approximation analysis of the factors which determine the level of employment.

[9] On the question of machines, Ricardo takes his central idea from Barton, who went so far as to write: "It is easy to conceive that, under certain circumstances, the whole of the annual savings of an industrious people might be added to fixed capital, in which case they would have no effect in increasing the demand for labour" (J. Barton, *Observations on the Circumstances which Influence the Conditions of the Labouring Classes of Society,* quoted in Ricardo, *Principles,* p. 396). Ricardo comments that "it is not easy . . . to conceive that under any circumstances an increase of capital should not be followed by an increased demand for labour; the most that can be said is that the demand will be in a diminishing ratio." Today, in the age of growing automation, the possibility which Barton envisaged does not appear quite so fantastic.

Labor-attracting and labor-repelling forces

When investment does not imply any changes in the technical coefficients, it is true, as Smith and Keynes assume, that an increase in investment raises the demand for labor and, hence, the employment level. When, by contrast, investment does imply a change in the coefficients, investment and employment may also vary in opposite directions, or investment may remain constant while employment falls.

We have already considered the first of these alternatives in the preceding chapter. This is the Ricardian case of increase in investment and decline of employment; we have seen that any unemployment originally generated by the introduction of additional machines can be reabsorbed only if investment and consumption expand. In actual fact, however, the other case — stability of investment, decline of employment — is also important and may occur even in the short period. What happens in this case is not that additional machines at once displace a certain number of workers, but that new and better machines are gradually substituted for old and worn-out ones. We propose to show that in this case, too, employment can return to its original level (or, if we consider the process resulting from contrasting forces, remain stable) only if investment and consumption rise.

Suppose that in the capital-goods ("machine") sector there are quality changes — an increase in the technical efficiency of each machine — without changes in the technical coefficients,[10] while in the consumer-goods sector technical coefficients are reduced. I have in mind especially a reduction in the labor coefficient due to the introduction of the new, improved machines. Suppose, furthermore, that despite the increase in the technical efficiency of machines their price remains unchanged. Suppose, finally, that the same number of machines continues to be produced, so that employment in the machine sector remains stable. Since these machines are now more efficient, they might enable firms in the consumer-goods sector to produce more without raising total employment and total money investment, simply by substituting new machines for the old ones as they wear out. In these circum-

[10] See p. 65–6.

stances, the higher productivity of the factors of production in the consumer-goods sector would benefit the income recipients (wage and profit earners), either through a fall in the prices of consumer goods or through an increase in money incomes. But these higher incomes can absorb the potential higher output if they are entirely spent on consumption. Only then can the firms in the consumer-goods sector translate the whole increment of productivity into higher output and thereby maintain both employment and money investment at their previous levels; otherwise these firms' investment and demand for labor diminish, with a consequent reduction of employment and of the money value of output in the machine sector, even though the latter's prices have not changed. If part of the higher incomes is saved, as normally happens, output of consumer goods increases less than productivity and employment falls. The question of the possible harmful effects of saving on employment is therefore, strictly speaking, meaningful only with reference to dynamic conditions. Stability of employment requires an expansion of the money demand not only for consumer goods but also for producer goods.

It follows that a rise in productivity generates forces which tend to displace workers from the productive process. Employment can then remain stable only if both consumption and total money investment grow. In short, and in extremely simplified terms, we may say that if productivity rises by, say, 3 percent annually and total money demand (gross national product, that is, the sum of consumption and gross money investment[11]) grows at a lower rate, the divergence will be translated into an increase in unemployment. Employment can remain stable only if total money demand rises at the same rate as productivity does, so that labor-attracting and labor-repelling forces offset each other.

Now, does this in fact happen? If so, in what conditions? Let us, for the moment, recall a few facts; later on we shall examine the question from the logical point of view.

Historically, no such compensation has ever taken place in a continuous fashion. Generally speaking, the attraction forces prevail in the prosperity phases of the cycle and the expulsion forces

---

[11] We neglect government expenditure for the time being.

during depression. As the individual firm installs its fixed plant in excess of normal sales just because of business fluctuations, so the normal level of employment in an economy which develops cyclically cannot be the level of full employment. Full employment has in the past been associated with the height of the boom, a situation which can in no way be considered "normal" or in a state of equilibrium. Hence, full employment, far from appearing as a characteristic of equilibrium, has always been a feature of unbalanced situations.[12]

We may recall in this context that the average level of unemployment in Great Britain between 1850 and 1914 was 5.5 percent of the labor force, and in the United States between 1890 and 1914 about 7 percent.[13]

In the interwar period the picture is rather confusing. The employment cycle with its surprising (and still unexplained) nearly regular recurrence can no longer be traced, and the level of employment was mainly depressed during most of that period. Such ups and downs as did occur can hardly be considered "cycles." With obvious reference to this period, Keynes notes that the economic system "seems capable of remaining in a chronic condition of sub-normal activity for a considerable period without any marked tendency either towards recovery or towards a complete collapse." [14]

It is often said that the years 1919–29 were on the whole prosperous ones, at least in the United States where we do indeed find

[12] This observation is implicit in Marco Fanno's and J. R. Hicks's later, independent, concept according to which the "potential upper limit of the upswing [Hicks's "full-employment ceiling"] is reached when all the unemployed have been reabsorbed." See Fanno, *La teoria delle fluttuazioni economiche* (Turin, 1947), p. 173; Hicks, *A Contribution to the Theory of the Trade Cycle* (Oxford, 1950). See also, Schumpeter, *Business Cycles,* I, 161.

[13] In Great Britain, during the years 1850–1914, the minimum level of unemployment was 1–2 percent in boom periods, and the maximum 12–13 percent in depression periods; in the United States, during the years 1890–1914, the minimum and maximum levels were 3–4 and 16–17 percent. The British figures are more reliable than the American ones. Prior to the dates of 1850 and 1890, respectively, we have only fragmentary figures pertaining to particular industries and no overall estimates. See A. C. Pigou, *Industrial Fluctuations* (London, 1929), pp. 381–2; P. Douglas, *Real Wages in the United States, 1890–1926* (Boston, 1928), p. 445.

[14] *General Theory,* p. 249.

symptoms of an almost feverish prosperity, fed in large part by stock-exchange speculation. But even in the United States these symptoms were accompanied by their opposites. Agriculture was already in a state of latent depression and the government began to intervene on a large scale to support farm prices.[15] Industrial firms were investing on a large scale, but more than two thirds of the total was "replacement investment" [16] of a kind which does not raise but reduces the demand for labor, and, during the years immediately preceding the collapse, a large part of total "investment" was purely speculative and not productive.[17] On the other hand, the boom owed much to private and public housing investment;[18] in spite of the population increase, the level of employment in manufacturing industry remained almost constant.[19]

The next ten years, 1929–39, need no comment. As is well known, unemployment in the United States reached the unprecedented level of over 20 percent. While the case of the United States during the first postwar decade is mixed, that of Europe is quite clear. All European economies were depressed during the

[15] See *The Structure of American Industry*, chap. 1, "Agriculture" by W. R. Knight, esp. pp. 32–7.

The farm crisis after the First World War has been attributed mainly to the great expansion of the area under cultivation during the war and to the disappearance of many outlets, especially on the European markets. These circumstances no doubt contributed much to the crisis, but its persistence (in a certain sense it is still with us today) and the long-term shifts in the relative prices of agriculture and industry suggest that agriculture was even then suffering from the effects of the same oligopolistic mechanism which is at work in contemporary industry. During the ten years following the First World War, industrial prices remained almost stationary, in spite of the cost reductions due to the tremendous rise in productivity. See Fanno, p. 147, and L. Einaudi, "Debiti," *Riforma sociale*, nos. 1–2 (1934), reprinted in L. Einaudi, *Nuovi saggi* (Turin, 1937), p. 58f. Einaudi writes (p. 68), with special reference to the American economy: "the slump which set in at the end of 1929 was due to the fact that prices had, *by some weird and unexplained magic,* remained stationary for too long and had thereby allowed an undue number of errors to accumulate" (my italics).

[16] A. H. Hansen, *Full Recovery or Stagnation?* (London, 1938), pp. 290–2.

[17] It has been calculated that in 1929 "productive" investment accounted for barely one fifth of corporate investment as a whole. See Schumpeter, *Business Cycles,* II, 879.

[18] Hansen, p. 292.

[19] *Historical Statistics of the United States, 1790–1944* (U. S. Department of Commerce, 1945), p. 65, col. 69. The unemployment figures are contradictory: those of the Department of Commerce (p. 65, cols. 62–5) are not very high, while Douglas (p. 427) gives very high ones.

entire interwar period.[20] In particular, unemployment throughout remained at a higher level than before the First World War.[21]
We conclude that during the interwar period the forces tending
to absorb labor were distinctly weaker than those tending to expel
labor. The employment cycle, which was so clear-cut before 1914,
can hardly be traced, while chronic unemployment became much
higher than it had been. It would seem that, while the problem
of the cycle had become less serious, a new and even more serious
problem had made its appearance: the problem of stagnation.

Keynes's equilibrium unemployment as a dynamic problem

These facts raise an important theoretical problem. If the
Smith-Keynes assumption, taken alone, is inadmissible even in
the short period, not because it is wrong but because it is partial
and therefore insufficient, how can we explain the persistence of
unemployment for such a long time?

If, together with Smith's assumption, we accept Ricardo's, as
Keynes seemed on the point of doing in 1930, we necessarily
leave the static view behind and begin to take a dynamic view.
The whole problem of underemployment equilibrium, or equilibrium unemployment, appears to be nonexistent as a static problem. We do not lose much by recognizing this. Both Modigliani[22]

[20] United Nations Economic Commission for Europe, *Growth and Stagnation
in the European Economy,* by I. Svennilson (Geneva, 1954), esp. chap. 3,
"Stagnation and Growth in the Interwar Period — A Summary of Findings."
    [21] For Great Britain, see Layton and Crowther, *An Introduction to the Study
of Prices,* pp. 265–6.
    [22] F. Modigliani, "Liquidity Preference and the Theory of Interest and
Money," *Econometrica,* 1944, reprinted in *Readings in Monetary Theory,* ed.
F. A. Lutz and L. W. Mints (Philadelphia, 1951).
    I should like to avail myself of this opportunity to express my gratitude
to Franco Modigliani, to whom I am indebted for an astute and stimulating
criticism of my article, "Monopoli, ristagno economico e politica keynesiana,"
in *Economia Internazionale,* November 1954. This was on the occasion of his
visit to Rome in 1955; subsequently, I have had more than one occasion to
discuss with Modigliani the whole question of the relationship between chronic
unemployment and monopolistic and oligopolistic formations. The criticism and
suggestions Modigliani communicated to me after perusal of the first edition of
this monograph enabled me to correct a number of mistakes and to introduce
improvements and clarifications in various places — especially in Chapter 2
(sections on "Long-Run Equilibrium in Concentrated Oligopoly" and "Some
Comments on the Model"), Chapter 5 ("Short-Run Price Rigidity"), Chapter
7 ("A Three-Sector Model").

TECHNOLOGICAL UNEMPLOYMENT 141

and Patinkin[23] reached, through different analyses, the conclusion that the Keynesian theory of equilibrium unemployment is tenable only on the assumption of wage rigidity — just as the neoclassical theory is, though for different reasons. Patinkin realized that static analysis was constitutionally unsuitable for the treatment of equilibrium unemployment and, at the end of his article, he called for dynamic analysis, without, however, putting forward more than vague suggestions and indications.

Now, if high and lasting unemployment is, contrary to appearances, not a static but a dynamic problem, then we must examine the "dynamic" forces which generate it. In line with Ricardo's assumption, what is necessary is a theoretical analysis of the two opposing forces which generate and absorb unemployment, with a view to explaining why and in what conditions the former may persistently tend to prevail over the latter.

A first line of approach to the treatment of chronic unemployment as a dynamic problem is suggested by the model we pre sented in the preceding chapter. The analysis of that model showed that the forces which tend to reabsorb the workers gradually liberated or made redundant by technical progress are weaker when the oligopolistic or monopolistic mechanism operates than when the mechanism of competition operates. This conclusion holds even when we suppose prices not to be perfectly rigid in relation to decreasing costs, but to be partially flexible, in the sense indicated more than once above.

To be more precise, we can state that, although the laborattracting forces do not cease to operate as oligopolistic and monopolistic formations spread (they continue to operate chiefly by way of the investment of profit), they tend to be overtaken by the labor-expelling forces — unless, as we shall see, an element outside private firms intervenes. This is public expenditure and investment.

If we admit that the process of concentration has made great advances, especially since the beginning of this century — so much so that it has created what is called "trustified capitalism" or, perhaps a better name, "oligopolistic capitalism" — and if we

[23] D. Patinkin, "Price Flexibility and Full Employment," *American Economic Review*, 1948, reprinted in *Readings in Monetary Theory*.

admit that the process of concentration logically leads to the spreading of "concentrated oligopoly," then we are led to formulate a first hypothesis to explain the stagnation of employment after the First World War: the forces tending to absorb unemployment were weakened because the field of action of the oligopolistic mechanism expanded at the expense of the classical mechanism of competition. Thus, our analysis so far appears to be useful in two ways. In general terms, it shows how different are the effects of technical progress on income and employment according as one or the other mechanism is in operation. In more specific terms, it offers a hypothesis for the explanation of the phenomenon which goes under the name of equilibrium unemployment. This, however, needs to be worked out somewhat more fully.

IX

Investment Opportunities
and Incentives

Generally speaking, we may distinguish three kinds of innovations according to their effects, which may be: (1) the production of new goods, (2) a change of the technical coefficients in the production of existing goods, and (3) a change in the quality of products. All these innovations create investment opportunities. In turn, there are three kinds of investment incentives: (1) a fall in factor prices, (2) a fall in the *sui generis* cost element represented by interest on loans, and (3) an expansion of demand.

Innovations, cost reductions, and expansion of demand

The importance of innovations as investment opportunities is generally recognized, but, apart from Schumpeter, nobody seems to have incorporated them organically into modern theory. At best, they appear as a sort of *deus ex machina* called "autonomous investment," that is, investment independent of any prior increase in demand. Similarly, the part played by a fall in factor prices as an investment incentive has been almost completely neglected.

We have already commented briefly on innovations leading to changes in the quality of products and shall presently dwell at some length on those leading to the production of new goods. A fall in the rate of interest will be discussed in Chapter 10. Meanwhile, let us take a brief look at the remaining investment opportunities and incentives.

Changes in technical coefficients leading to cost reductions in the production of existing goods may be due to major innovations (the conditions for the introduction of which will be examined below) or to technical improvements, which may be considered minor innovations. The latter fall properly within the category which Marshall describes as internal economies.[1] The Marshallian long-run supply curve thus incorporates, and thereby hides,[2] one of the investment incentives.

A cost reduction due to innovations or technical improvements leads in the long period to a corresponding price reduction if competition prevails in the branches where such a cost reduction takes place; under oligopoly or monopoly, prices do not fall or at least fall less than proportionately. When the prices in question are those of factors of production, this diminishes the effectiveness of one of the investment incentives.

A *fall in the prices of factors of production* also works unconditionally as an investment incentive under competition; under monopoly, it works either not at all or only to a limited extent; and under oligopoly, it works mainly when the prices which fall are those of the variable factors. In that case the prices of finished goods are reduced proportionately and, if this leads to an expansion of demand, the entrepreneurs have an inducement to invest. This type of investment incentive is especially important in those branches of production where, for technical reasons, there is not much scope for innovation.

There is a fundamental difference among the various market forms as regards the connection between a change in technical coefficients and a fall in factor prices and as regards the ultimate consequences of the former. Suppose that costs fall as a result of a change in technical coefficients due to some innovation or technical improvement. Under competition, such cost reductions are followed by corresponding price reductions. If the goods whose prices fall are used as factors of production in a large

[1] *Principles*, Book V, chap. 12, pgh. 3: "[In considering the long-period supply price] we exclude from view any economies that may result from substantive new inventions; but we include those which may be expected to arise naturally out of adaptations of existing ideas." The objection that this view is incompatible with the static hypothesis seems fully justified.

[2] If we want to take account not only of economies of scale but also of technical improvements, we have to construct different long-period supply curves, or, what amounts to the same thing, if we wish to consider only one curve, we have to say that this curve shifts downward as time goes on.

number of firms and therefore enter into their costs, the price fall will set in motion the chain of repercussions which we have examined and will, directly or indirectly, create investment incentives in many firms. Under oligopoly, on the other hand, and *a fortiori* under monopoly, investment incentives of this kind are created only in special circumstances and hence to a limited extent. Since prices do not necessarily fall as a result of cost reductions due to innovations which change the technical coefficients, the effects of any particular innovation may not spread beyond the branches where it is introduced, and investment incentives due to a fall in factor prices fail to appear or appear only to a limited extent. Yet, as we have seen, it is principally investment induced by a fall in factor prices which releases the forces tending to absorb unemployment and raise real income. The diffusion of oligopolistic and monopolistic formations causes the chances of absorption of unemployment to depend more and more on the remaining investment incentive: expansion of demand.

Expansion of demand (a shift of the demand curve to the right) stimulates investment in any market form; but in conditions of concentrated oligopoly the expansion of demand must be sufficiently large to allow firms to overcome the obstacle of technological discontinuities. An expansion of demand stimulates investment even when the technical coefficients, and therefore costs, do not change. New factories identical with existing ones can be set up and prices need not change at all. As we have seen (Chapter 3), this tends to happen in mature and well-established industries, provided, of course, that factor prices do not change.

Major innovations

In conditions of oligopoly and monopoly, expansion of demand also conditions the type of innovations which will be introduced.

Innovations consisting of radical technical transformations imply a considerable increase in the innovating firms' annual investment. This increase is usually due to the introduction of new machines which are much more expensive than the previous ones; expenditures for other factors of production, including labor, may rise, remain unchanged, or fall. If they rise or remain unchanged, or if they fall by less than the increment in the machine investment — that is, if total cost rises — production must increase because this is the only way of producing at lower average costs. But any firm whose output is large enough not to be negligible in relation to total output must consider the question of probable price changes. If it is thought that the larger output can be absorbed by the market only at prices which are so much lower than the initial ones that they make an inroad on annual profits, then the firm will conclude that it is not profitable to introduce the innovation. In other words, the introduction of the innovation depends upon the elasticity of demand.[3] It may be said, of course, that oligopolistic firms do not know, and perhaps cannot know, the elasticity of demand and that their investment decisions are guided by estimates of the probable rate of change, and more especially the rate of expansion, of demand at unchanged prices. We are thus led to conclude that investment in major innovations is essentially conditioned by the rate of expansion of demand.[4]

Let us now consider innovations which actually create new industries producing new goods. If the minimum investment necessary to apply the new technique is relatively small, the innovating firm will quickly be followed by imitators; in other words, we may get Schumpeterian competition. But if the mini-

---

[3] This case is discussed in detail in my article in the November 1954 issue of *Economia Internazionale*. See also S. Lombardini, *Il monopolio nella teoria economica* (Milan, 1953), pp. 189–91.

[4] With reference to stationary demand conditions and arguing on the basis of the concept of the kinked demand curve, Oskar Lange (*Price Flexibility and Employment*, pp. 75–6) reached the following conclusion, which is not far from my own: "Under oligopoly, an innovation cannot be output-increasing unless the diminution of marginal cost caused by it is sufficiently great to induce the firm to break the 'discipline' of the group. The last-mentioned case happens when the marginal-cost curve shifts to such an extent as to make it get out of the range of discontinuity of the marginal-revenue curve. Thus, only innovations that reduce marginal cost to a great extent can be output-increasing under conditions of oligopoly. It follows that, unless it causes a sufficiently large reduction of marginal cost . . . an innovation cannot be, under oligopoly, all-around factor-using, or even all-around factor-neutral; it must 'save' at least some factor at some date in the firm's production plan. Except with regard to innovations that *greatly* reduce marginal cost . . . oligopoly exerts a selective action against output-increasing and in favor of factor-saving innovations."

mum investment is large and if it is clear from the outset that only a considerable volume of demand can make the innovation profitable, then the new industry will be concentrated, since it is protected from the very beginning by a technological, and therefore economic, discontinuity. Considering how difficult it is to start from scratch in setting up a large firm, which in this case cannot develop out of an existing smaller one,[5] it is most likely that the production of the new good will be undertaken by an existing large firm already operating in some other branch (see p. 61).

Some indication, however uncertain, of the probable size of the market for the new product — that is, the economic space that can be conquered — is given by the extent of demand for existing goods satisfying needs similar to those which can be satisfied by the new product, as well as by the tendential rate of increase of demand for those existing goods.

The consequences of innovation and Schumpeter's business-cycle theory

In considering the consequences of major innovations and innovations leading to the production of new goods, we have to recall briefly some aspects of Schumpeter's model. In this model, we have first the appearance of an entrepreneur who produces existing goods by new methods, or new goods, and then the appearance of a group of imitators, other entrepreneurs who try to do what the innovator has done and to obtain the same profits. In this manner investment grows and, as a result, demand for finished products expands and the cyclical upswing develops. The boom is followed by recession as the fruits of innovation mature and as there is an increase in the output of those firms which do not innovate but simply take advantage of the general prosperity. The recession begins precisely at the moment when the wave of higher output breaks on the market, and it is due to the simultaneous processes of autodeflation, or the repayment of debts by firms, and to the total or almost total cessation of credit creation. Prices fall and the less efficient firms go bankrupt.

[5] According to Marshall, large and very large firms always have small origins; the trees of the forest must have been saplings once.

Recession turns into depression. The fall in prices, which to some extent is lasting, causes real incomes to rise because money incomes fall less than prices. (There are some obvious points of resemblance here with classical analysis.)

This model may be fairly realistic and possess a good deal of explanatory value with reference to an economy where industry is not highly concentrated, where small firms predominate and the entry of new firms — hence also of the imitators — is relatively easy. But the model needs to be radically changed if it is to apply to an economy where industry has reached a high degree of concentration. Schumpeter himself realized this; he spoke of the last century's competitive capitalism in contrast to our century's prevailing trustified capitalism (or, as I would prefer to say, oligopolistic capitalism) and was led to observe that to take account of this kind of change, "many details — in some points more than details — would . . . have to be altered in our model." [6] But in actual fact Schumpeter did not, in 1939, greatly modify the model which he had worked out before the First World War.[7]

Some of the characteristics of the cycle which Schumpeter analyzed and which I have recalled in extremely brief form do not exist today. In many branches of industry there is no longer any possibility for imitators to enter the market or, at any rate, this possibility exists only at a very high level, that is, for very large concentrated concerns which invade each others' markets and compete in an entirely new sense. There is a fundamental difference between the economic consequences of major innovations at the time of competitive capitalism and those in our own age of oligopolistic capitalism, and this difference may perhaps best be described as follows. Given that technological innovations are now initiated, in great and growing measure, by existing large concerns rather than by new firms,[8] these

---

[6] *Business Cycles,* p. 96.

[7] Curiously enough, Schumpeter seemed more inclined to stress the importance of structural transformations in the modern economy, and their effects on business cycles, when he wrote his *Theory of Economic Development* in 1911 than he was when he wrote *Business Cycles* in 1939. See Sylos-Labini, "Il problema dello sviluppo economico in Marx ed in Schumpeter."

[8] Schumpeter, *Theory of Economic Development,* p. 67.

innovations do not necessarily lead to additional investment, as they do in Schumpeter's model. The existing large firms can carry out innovations simply by making a new kind of investment *in place* of another which would have been made on the basis of the old methods of production; any increase in the actual volume of investment in connection with innovations is purely fortuitous. In the past, "the new" was additional and in competition with "the old," and the necessary increase in the volume of investment implied an increase in total money demand and consequently a general expansion of economic activity. Today the new is not necessarily additional to the old but as often as not replaces it gradually: thus the volume of investment need not necessarily grow even if productivity rises. In modern conditions major innovations and innovations leading to the production of new goods can be controlled by the large firms already operating either in the industry to which the innovation applies or in industries with related technologies, all the more so when the innovation requires not only large initial investment but also, as happens more and more often, well-equipped research laboratories and experienced teams of technicians and specialized workers.

The large firms will use their power of control over major innovations in such a manner as to space out their introduction with a view to minimizing business losses due to premature obsolescence of the existing machines. In the past, when the entry of new firms was easy, no such distribution over time was possible; in the presence of multiple decision centers, the "new" could not gradually replace the "old" but had to compete with it and find its place alongside it. One of the most important consequences of the new situation is that the great wave of bankruptcies which used to spread during recession and depression is now much weaker.[9] Bankruptcies are now limited to such sectors as retail trade, where small and very small firms are still the rule.[10]

Another consequence is that in oligopolistic capitalism the highly concentrated industries become more and more independ-

[9] I owe this observation to Paul Rosenstein-Rodan.
[10] We may also note, incidentally, that this fact tends to diminish capital losses and hence to reduce the capital/output ratio for the economy as a whole.

ent of bank credits and the creation of bank money, since the large firms can finance all or most innovations out of depreciation charges and profits, the latter being high in overall terms and often also in unit terms (see below).

Finally, yet another characteristic of the old business cycle is gradually disappearing: the price fall during recession. Even during the recessions of the relatively prosperous first half of the interwar period, prices remained almost constant,[11] and since the last war this phenomenon has become very clear-cut. In the highly concentrated industries recession is no longer accompanied by a price drop, and in some important cases we have witnessed price rises.[12]

Innovations, investment, and unemployment

While major innovations necessitate an increase in the total volume of investment, minor innovations do not. The latter can be introduced through normal replacement of machines (see Chapter 8) and can be financed out of gradually accumulating depreciation funds. Even major innovations can to a large extent be financed in the same manner when they are spaced out over time by the large firms.

If total demand increases at a sufficiently high rate, it will be to the advantage of the large firms to introduce all kinds of innovations, even those which imply an increase in total cost. Both old and new machines can then be utilized and the question of obsolescence does not arise, or at any rate is not decisive. Total cost rises, but output rises more and, thanks to growing demand, can be sold at unchanged prices. Employment does not fall. If, on the other hand, demand rises slowly or not at all, oligopolistic firms tend to invest only in minor innovations, which do not raise total cost and can be financed out of depreciation funds. The average productivity of labor then still rises, but unemployment also tends to rise.

All in all we can say that, in an economy where oligopolistic formations are spreading, depreciation funds in the long run ac-

[11] See above, p. 139 n. 15.
[12] See above, p. 73.

quire growing importance as a source of investment financing by firms. This tendency is very plain in the United States, even in conditions of expanding demand, as in recent years. Thus, "Depreciation charges have risen to the forefront among available corporate funds in the postwar period, constituting the largest single source of financing over the last 8 years. This growing importance is illustrated in the increase of its share from one-fourth of total financing requirements in 1950 to nearly one-half in 1957." [13]

In conditions of stationary demand, the tendency for innovations to be almost entirely financed out of depreciation funds is equally clear, both in Great Britain and in the United States during the 1930s. For Great Britain, we have Colin Clark's testimony in 1936:

The very rapid expansion in productivity of the present time is taking place at a time of heavily diminishing capital accumulation. . . . Without new investment the replacement of obsolete capital . . . appears to give all the necessary scope for the introduction of technical and organizational improvement, and to bring about the rapid increase in productivity under which we are now living.[14]

With reference to the same period in the United States, A. H. Hansen writes:

I have frequently called attention to the remarkable fact that of the 60 billion dollars of gross capital formation in business plant and equipment made in the decade 1931–1940, 90 per cent was replacement investment. Yet even though there was relatively little *net* investment, the productive capacity of American industry was enormously greater at the end of the decade than it was in 1930. Better and more productive equipment was installed in place of the worn-out and discarded equipment.[15]

Thus, stationary demand means stationary total investment and increasing unemployment, while the average productivity of labor may go on rising quite as much as it does in periods of expanding demand. Since in these conditions depreciation funds

---

[13] H. I. Liebling, "Financing Business in Recession and Expansion," *Survey of Current Business,* October 1958, pp. 17–18 (Table 3).
[14] *National Income and Outlay* (London, 1937), p. 272.
[15] *Monetary Theory and Fiscal Policy* (New York, 1949), p. 111.

are enough to finance innovations, the undistributed corporate profits of oligopolistic and monopolistic firms tend to be hoarded, or in any case not invested.

Technical progress and the large oligopolistic firm

The large oligopolistic firm, considered individually, can be and often is technically superior to the necessarily small competitive firm. It seems almost to work miracles. Its research laboratories produce results not only of practical but of high scientific value; its own larger financial resources and its greater creditworthiness enable it to invest on a scale well beyond the reach of any single small competitive firm; it can also pay, and often finds it profitable to pay, higher wages than other firms.

The truth of these observations must be obvious to anyone who looks about him with open eyes. Economists seem to have an undue fondness and regard for certain simple formulas, for otherwise it would be hard to explain why so many of them found (and some still find) it difficult not only to analyze these facts but even to acknowledge them — and this after the facts have been brought to light over and over again and were so forcefully presented by Schumpeter.

The social problem which oligopolistic concentration creates is not that individual large oligopolistic firms stand in the way of technical progress, for, when all is said and done, in this respect they deserve Schumpeter's praise. Nor is it that they pay their workers low wages. The social problem of oligopoly ultimately originates outside the single oligopolistic firm, or at any rate outside its technical organization. The problem resides in the oligopolistic firms' price and cost policies, in the particular way in which the fruits of technical progress achieved by oligopolistic firms are distributed throughout the economy, and in the imbalance which this distribution creates. Last but not least, there is the grave social problem of chronic and general unemployment due to the weakening of the forces which tend to absorb labor released by mechanization.

What, if anything, can be done to relieve and remove such unemployment in an economy dominated by oligopolistic formations? This is the question to which Part Three will be devoted. Generally speaking, we have seen that, provided total demand expands at a sufficient rate, all kinds of investment are feasible and chronic unemployment may remain tolerably low. The question which will occupy us, then, is *how* total demand can grow.

Individually, the performance of large oligopolistic firms may be, and undoubtedly often is, superior to that of competitive firms; but *in the social context* they create new problems. If we want to discover the new problems and new tendencies which are associated with oligopoly and are alien to competition, we may legitimately compare the behavior of firms in conditions of oligopoly (and monopoly) and in conditions of competition. Only in these terms is it logically sound and analytically useful to compare firms operating under different market forms. If we speak of the new problems of the oligopolistic era, we do not wish to imply (as we hope will be quite clear at this stage) that we have any nostalgia for what Schumpeter calls the imaginary golden age of the past, when competition reigned supreme and all was well in the best of all possible worlds. First of all, we should refer not to neoclassical "perfect competition," which never existed anywhere, but to classical competition, conceived as a dynamic process characterized by relative ease of entry of new firms. Second, we have to remember that although, historically, certain problems and tendencies were absent or had less weight in the age of competition, it knew others which we are spared — much more poverty and the ruthless exploitation of female and child labor, to name only two.

The question of self-financing

The superior performance of large oligopolistic firms (considered individually) in comparison with competitive firms has been debated and discussed from different angles. One of the reasons often advanced for it is the higher self-financing capacity of oligopolistic firms. We also hear much talk of the positive effects of self-financing on economic development. This is a question which repays some careful attention.

Self-financing, or the financing of a firm's productive development by its own funds, means that the firm plows back its profits. When self-financing becomes a continuous process, we have to ask ourselves how firms obtain their profits.

In conditions of competition, continuous self-financing is possible only if costs are steadily reduced. "Extraordinary" profits permit self-financing for a short while: they are transitory, just because prices tend to fall in accordance with cost reductions. Normal profits allow only very little room for self-financing when the firms are small, as they are in a competitive market.

In conditions of monopoly and oligopoly, by contrast, continuous self-financing may rest on a permanent and considerable gap between costs and prices. If costs fall, prices are reduced less than proportionally, or not at all; as a consequence, there is a rise both in wages and in profits, which are the source of self-financing. It follows that the self-financing capacity of monopolistic or oligopolistic firms may be, and generally is, higher than that of competitive firms. But this higher capacity takes the place of a price fall, or, in other words, it comes about at the expense of that chain of positive reactions which we discussed in Chapter 7. Self-financing continuously nourished by prices in excess of costs is therefore a very different and, from the point of view of society as a whole, a very much less advantageous matter than self-financing nourished by transitory extraordinary profits that are soon wiped out by price reductions and are re-created only if costs are reduced again.[16]

To the extent that long-run price flexibility can be increased at all in conditions of monopoly and oligopoly — and up to a certain point it can be increased [17] — it would obviously be desirable to do so. It is true that this would diminish the large firms' self-financing capacity and would force them to draw more heavily on credits, but society as a whole would gain thereby.[18]

[16] See A. Breglia, "Profitti sterili e profitto fecondo," *Giornale degli economisti*, May 1953.

[17] At least to the extent that price rigidity is not structural, but due to such "artificial" elements as tariff protection, official price supports, or legal cartels. See Chapter 7.

[18] These reflections are largely the result of a conversation I had with Professor Giorgio Fuà. The discussion makes it clear that we are here considering the problems of price determination and the financing of the firm's produc-

The process of concentration and the two types of oligopoly

The above arguments of "superiority" obviously apply to the firms which are typical of a situation of concentrated oligopoly. It remains a fact that the process of concentration is essentially due to the pursuit of higher technical efficiency and to the tendency to produce at decreasing costs. Now, as in the past, the process is essentially one of the creation of large and efficient productive units, and the resulting market forms are constitutionally different from competition. New problems arise which did not exist when competition was the rule, or which at any rate were much less serious. Nevertheless — and this cannot be repeated too often — there is no doubt whatever that the new firms represent enormous progress in comparison with the small firms of the past.

Though this is certainly true of the production units typical of concentrated oligopoly, the situation may be, and often is, very different in markets where differentiated oligopoly prevails. The more differentiated the products are, the more difficult it is to introduce those modern mass-production methods which are the main source of both continual cost reductions and the process of concentration. Product differentiation may thus be an obstacle to concentration no less than it is to cost reductions.[19] In other words, it would seem that historically and empirically there is an antinomy between the two market forms of concentrated and differentiated oligopoly which conceptually have so much in common.

These considerations suggest that if we want to arrive at valid conclusions about the efficiency and, more generally, the behavior of firms, it is not enough simply to consider the market form under which they operate. We have to consider the market form and the technological conditions together.

---

tive development as aspects of the overall problem of general economic development. I recommend this matter to the attention of students of welfare economics.

[19] This is very clear in the case of small shops and in the commerce of highly differentiated agricultural products.

Part Three

EFFECTIVE DEMAND
AND ECONOMIC STAGNATION

X

The Problem of Effective Demand

In an economy with little concentration, where the entry of new firms is relatively easy and the market form is, therefore, largely competitive, no entrepreneur controls enough output to have to worry about total demand. Each firm's investment decisions are based on price, which the entrepreneur cannot alter, and on cost, which he can modify only to the extent that he manages to change the technical coefficients through better production methods (he cannot influence factor prices). A firm will invest on two conditions: it must have some funds of its own, since it cannot finance its investment entirely on credit, and it must be able to produce, or to expand production, at costs which are lower than price, in order to earn at least what is considered a normal profit. If production expands because of a great deal of new investment and prices eventually fall, there is nothing the individual firm can do about it. The less efficient firms, which produce at the highest cost, go bankrupt and disappear from the market. (In competition, exit is as "easy" as entry.) In a competitive economy a prolonged price depression is therefore perfectly compatible with growth of national product in real terms.[1] This was, indeed, a familiar development over long stretches of the past century.[2] In our century's highly concentrated economies this can no longer happen. Prices may fall, of course, and they do for a relatively long time, but then output necessarily also

[1] However, national product in money terms (which is an expression of total money demand) and total money investment may fall if the decline in prices is faster than the increase in the volume of output.

[2] Especially in the 1820s and 30s, 1870s, 1880s, and part of the 1890s. Some economists, like Schumpeter, maintain that prices had a basic falling trend right through the century.

falls or stagnates, as happened, for instance, in the 1930s. Today many and important markets are dominated by large firms, which do — and must — think in terms of their own market's total demand. It is not enough that these firms should have disposable funds from their own and other sources, or that they should be able to produce at costs lower than the price at any given moment. Just because they are large and because changes in their output necessarily have an influence on prices, these firms invest and expand production only when they believe they can count on growing money demand and thus on expanding sales at constant or only slightly reduced prices, which would assure them of growing total profits.

Demand and market form

The investments of competitive firms are basically limited by disposable funds, those of oligopolistic and monopolistic firms by demand. Although the simple formulas expressing the equilibrium position of competitive, monopolistic, and oligopolistic firms are no more than a first approximation, they do at least show that under monopoly and oligopoly, but not under competition, demand enters directly into the equilibrium conditions of the firm.[3]

Here we are reminded of two of Ricardo's fundamental propositions. The first is that under competition the individual firm's accumulation is limited only by the level of profit, which depends on the level of prices and costs, especially wages; and profit supplies both the motive and the funds for accumulation. The second is that the equilibrium price under competition depends on cost and under monopoly on supply and demand; this is true of competition also, but only "for a limited period."[4] Demand may, of

[3] I have in mind the formulas $p = m$ (for competition), $p - (p/\eta) = m$ (for monopoly), and $p = v + qv$ or, if direct cost equals marginal cost, $p = m + qm$ (for oligopoly), where q depends jointly on the elasticity of demand, the absolute size of the market, the state of technology, and possibly on initial selling expenditure.

[4] In chapter 30 of his Principles, Ricardo refutes Say and Lauderdale, who maintain that price depends on supply and demand in all cases, by adducing the example of a cost reduction in the production of an agricultural commodity on the assumption of unchanged demand: the cost reduction is sufficient to

course, indirectly influence the investment decisions of competitive firms. Growing demand (in cyclical recovery and boom) creates favorable conditions for the entry of new firms and, more important, causes prices and, hence, profits and investable funds to rise. As a result, the basic limit to the investment of competitive firms becomes less restrictive.

The small firms which do business alongside the large ones in relatively highly concentrated oligopolistic branches are, in certain respects, in much the same position as competitive firms. Their investment decisions, too, are governed by disposable funds and by the relation between cost and a price which they cannot influence, and they can also be indirectly affected by demand insofar as it may cause profits and investable funds to grow. However, unlike competitive firms, the small firms in a concentrated market are, in addition, subject to the influence of the large firms' policy. If the size of the market grows and the large firms merely intend to keep their market share, the field of action of the small firms broadens and they can expand in proportion with the market, without fear of reprisals.

We see that in a highly concentrated economy effective demand becomes the principal regulatory element of employment. Moreover, not only the volume of demand but also its composition is apt to create difficulties for the growth of investment and employment. A highly concentrated economy is, in practice, also a highly industrialized one. In such an economy, personal incomes are high and a large proportion of consumer expenditure is directed to products other than subsistence goods. As a consequence, states Alfred E. Kahn, "demand becomes unreliable, requires stimulation, may fluctuate within wide limits. And much of demand becomes postponable, because it is for consumer durables, replacements for which can be postponed, and because it is for instruments of production, demand for which, especially in a private enterprise economy (where investment depends on

---

lead to a price reduction. On rereading this chapter of the *Principles*, it seems almost incomprehensible how Ricardo should so often have been reproached for neglecting demand as an element which, together with cost, determines "value." Marshall's defense (*Principles of Economics*, Appendix I) of Ricardo against Jevons does more to obscure the question than to clarify it.

uncertainties, incentives, vagaries of psychology, innovation), may fluctuate widely." [5]

The problem of excessive saving

Because the investment decisions of large firms are decisively influenced by demand, it may happen that disposable funds exceed the requirements of self-financing. Since profit taxes constitute an external datum for the firm and since dividends have to be paid whether business is good or bad, varying but little in the short run, disposable funds are a residual. [6]

These funds may be invested to raise the firm's own productive capacity; but if the firm decides not to plow back all its disposable funds because it cannot see sufficient demand ahead to guarantee a profitable market for increased output, these funds may, at least in part, be otherwise employed. They may be deposited with banks or invested in other firms. But they may also be kept as a cash reserve or used for the repayment of debts; they may be used merely to extend the firm's financial control over other companies, for example, by mergers; or they may find their way into some sort of speculative stock-market trans-

[5] These observations were addressed to me in 1955 by Alfred Kahn in a letter commenting upon my thesis, then barely embryonic, regarding the relation between monopoly, oligopoly, and effective demand. Professor Kahn made it clear that he regarded the idea expressed by his observations as an alternative explanation. More precisely, he thought that if the problem of effective demand had recently become serious enough to worry everybody, this was not so much because of the process of concentration and oligopolistic formations, but rather because of the high level of average personal incomes. But it would seem that the two aspects, size and composition of demand, are complementary rather than mutually exclusive.

To Professor Kahn, too, I would like to acknowledge a debt of gratitude for many long and stimulating discussions, in writing and personal conversations. I am especially grateful to him for the criticisms he addressed to me after perusal of the 1956 edition of this monograph, which enabled me to make notable improvements, especially in Chapter 3 (sections on "Changes in Technology" and "Variations of Direct Costs and Prices during Prosperity"), Chapter 5 ("Unit Profits"), Chapter 7 ("A Three-Sector Model"), Chapter 9 ("The Process of Concentration and the Two Types of Oligopoly").

[6] This argument was fully developed by J. R. Meyer and E. Kuh in *The Investment Decision: An Empirical Study* (Cambridge, Mass., 1957), and was first briefly mentioned by L. Tarshis in "The Flow of Business Funds, Consumption and Investment," in *Post-Keynesian Economics*, ed. K. K. Kurihura (New Brunswick, 1954).

action. All these uses may be advantageous or profitable for the firm, but they are not investment in the proper sense of the word: they do not increase productive capacity anywhere in the economy. Nor do they cause effective demand to grow; on the contrary, in some cases they may reduce it.

Thus we are faced with a problem of savings, in terms which recall Keynes's; but the problem arises not from "psychological motives" but from the objective conditions which govern the managerial decisions of large firms and which are, in the last analysis, connected with the broad question of outlets in highly concentrated markets.[7]

Keynes's psychological motives may seem to be relevant for personal saving, but this statement needs very important qualifications. First of all, in recent years numerous investigations concerning personal saving have shown that both the marginal and the average propensity to save are conditioned not so much by purely subjective motives deriving from some abstract concept of immutable "human nature" as by objective and measurable economic and social factors, such as the highest income previously earned, the saver's position in the income distribution of a group, or changes over time in the stream of personal income. These factors are, of course, anything but constant and immutable. Second, we have to remember that personal saving nowadays accounts for only a small part of total saving and falls far short of corporate and public saving.[8] Finally, personal saving tends to become institutionalized through the diffusion of insurance and pension schemes, all of which tend to straighten out the income stream over time. In these circumstances, personal savings are administered in much the same way as corporate and public savings.

However, having said all this about the "motives" of saving, we can accept Keynes's conclusion that personal saving depends principally on the level of income and is not sensitive to changes

[7] In the case of corporate saving, as in the case of public saving, the irrelevance of "psychological motives" is immediately obvious, as G. Haberler has rightly pointed out (*Prosperity and Depression*, p. 228f).

[8] Tarshis shows that in recent years United States corporate saving was roughly two to three times as much as personal saving, and public saving was about twice as much again as corporate saving (see n. 6).

in the rate of interest. A fall in the rate of interest does not necessarily mean a reduction in the supply of personal savings and a corresponding increase in consumption.

Apart from corporate and personal saving, there is, of course, public saving effected by governmental and public authorities, mainly by means of taxation. Quantitatively, this is by far the largest category today. We shall have more to say about this later. Neglecting government saving for the moment, we note the existence of a Keynesian savings problem: the formation and variations of corporate and personal savings are independent of variations in the rate of interest, and they may tend to exceed investment, which in its turn depends more and more on variations in demand.

Investment, effective demand, and credit policy

Concentration in the banking sector, which has been even more rapid than industrial concentration,[9] has greatly increased the central bank's power to control the entire banking system. In turn, this has enhanced the government's power to control the whole body of monetary and credit policy through the central bank, and, having this power, governments have been compelled to exercise it in times of crisis and depression. Government became "the monetary authority." [10]

The implications of these developments on the effectiveness of monetary and credit policy were amply examined on many occasions during the first half of this century. These studies, most of which took their inspiration from Wicksell's monetary analysis, had a practical purpose: to find ways and means of shortening cyclical downswing and depression and to reduce the amplitude of fluctuations. Two oft-discussed questions were whether the greater power of control over money and credit was matched by a corresponding ability to influence the volume of investment, and whether the most suitable instrument for this purpose was the bank rate. It seemed obvious that the answer to both questions was in the affirmative, and the authors of most of these

[9] See M. Fanno, *Lezioni di economia e di scienza bancaria* (Padua, 1937).
[10] See A. Breglia, *L'economia dal punto di vista monetario* (3rd ed., Rome, 1951), esp. pp. 259–60, 327–30.

studies did, in fact, arrive at this conclusion. But they could do so only because they assumed explicitly or, more often, implicitly the existence of perfect competition not only on commodity but also on credit markets. In a competitive commodity market, as we have seen above, the firm decides to expand production, and hence to invest, in the light of prices (which it cannot influence), costs, and disposable funds. If the credit market is a perfect market, demand for loans is homogeneous and its variations depend solely on the rate of interest. On the assumption that perfect competition prevails in all markets, it is therefore legitimate to maintain that the demand for loanable funds and their supply are governed solely by the level of the rate of interest. But if we admit that in reality conditions are generally very far from perfect competition, the whole discussion has to be reopened.

Keynes — repeating, with slight modifications, a neoclassical proposition — says that investment continues up to the point where the marginal efficiency of capital (the expected profit rate) equals the rate of interest. This is true only in conditions of competition. Under monopoly, a reduction in the rate of interest may have no influence whatever on investment decisions. Under concentrated oligopoly, the large firms are financed largely by their own funds, and the level of the rate of interest has little bearing on their investment decisions.

Changes in the rate of interest may have an effect on the investments of small firms operating either in a not highly concentrated branch or alongside large firms in a highly concentrated one; this is particularly true of such industries as building, where interest is an important cost element. These changes may also have an effect on the composition of investment, insofar as they modify the cost of keeping inventories, independently of the conditions of the market in which the firm operates. Finally, interest changes may have an effect on credits to consumers. But in prevalently oligopolistic industries the effect of interest changes on the volume of investment, and thereby on production, cannot be more than slight; demand is the dominating factor.[11]

[11] If, in a highly concentrated market, the fall in the rate of interest is sharp and enduring enough to reduce the cost of inventories for all firms, even though in different degrees, it leads to a general cost reduction, which in its turn (see

These observations on the relationship between rate of interest and investment correspond to now generally accepted conclusions.[12]

The imperfections of the credit market are seen in the varying degrees of difficulty which firms, at a given interest rate, experience in obtaining bank credits — to the point, sometimes, of being unable to obtain any credit at all. In these circumstances, the level of the rate of interest is not the only relevant factor on the credit market; the banks' willingness to lend or, in other words, the degree to which the banking system's credit policy is liberal or restrictive acquires importance. This is again a problem which concerns primarily the small firms, whose self-financing potential for expansion is limited.

Thus, both variations in the rate of interest and the restrictive or liberal nature of banking policy affect mainly small firms. Since large firms carry far and away the greatest weight in modern industry and small firms are most often directly or indirectly subordinated to the large firms' policies, we are led to conclude that, on the whole, credit policy has little influence on the volume of investment. In any event, it is well to remember that countercyclical credit restrictions principally affect small firms — either indirectly, through higher interest rates, or directly, through a reduction in the credits granted.

Spontaneous expansion of demand

We have said that in a predominantly oligopolistic or monopolistic economy all investments can increase, including those which raise the demand for labor, if demand expands at a sufficiently high rate. In the presence of the latter condition, unemployment can gradually be absorbed. But how can demand expand? In particular, how can it expand spontaneously, that is, without government intervention?

Chapter 3) tends to cause price reductions and so to stimulate demand. The increased demand may stimulate investment. In oligopoly, then, any effect which a fall in the rate of interest may have on investment is indirect. If it takes place at all, it takes place by way of an expansion of demand. If demand fails to expand when prices fall, investment does not expand.

[12] See *Oxford Studies in the Price Mechanism,* chap. 1, "The Rate of Interest" (essays by R. S. Sayers, H. D. Henderson, J. E. Meade, P. W. S. Andrews, and A. J. Brown).

Many economists have pointed to population growth as one of the main causes generating an expansion of demand. But the connection is not immediate. Unless the new labor force finds its place in the productive apparatus and so earns additional incomes, population growth generates an increase not in demand but in poverty.

In the first place, demand can expand when productivity increases, so that incomes (profits and wages) rise and, with them, demand. However, as we have noted earlier (Chapter 8), the entire income increment is not consumed — part of it is saved. Therefore, although an expansion in the demand for consumer goods makes it possible to expand production, it is not enough to keep employment stable. The difficulty may be attenuated to some extent by a relatively greater increase of wages than of profits because wage earners have a lower propensity to save than profit earners. It is true, as will be seen when we examine the concrete example of the American economy, that an expansion in the demand for consumer goods (and especially services) through higher productivity does contribute to the development of the system; but it is not, and cannot be, sufficient in itself to prevent an increase in unemployment.

Demand can grow, in the second place, when new firms are created or existing firms expand. This leads directly to an increase in the demand for capital goods and indirectly, through the multiplier, to an increase in consumer demand.

Third, demand can expand as a result of the introduction of major innovations. In the nature of things, innovations of this kind are largely unpredictable and so are their effects. It may well happen that monopolistic or oligopolistic firms introduce such innovations without the inducement of an already rising demand. In this case total demand may spontaneously expand to the extent necessary to keep employment stable. However, as we have seen, not even major innovations can be introduced by the large firms without some sort of reference to the size of the potential market — which means considering both the size of the market for goods similar to the new ones to be produced as the result of the innovation and the size the market must be to make the innovation profitable. Investment occasioned by these innovations is, therefore, not nearly so "autonomous" as many seem to think. At certain times, when technological progress is particularly marked, investment called forth by major innovations does help to generate a spontaneous expansion of demand sufficient to offset the labor-repelling forces and to raise employment. But we must at once add the qualification that in a highly concentrated economy occasions of this kind are more subject to limiting factors and, therefore, tend to become rarer than they are in a less concentrated economy.

The facts are that, in the presence of technical progress, employment can remain stable or rise only if there is an expansion not merely in consumption but also in investment. As oligopolistic and monopolistic formations continue to spread, such an increase in investment comes more and more to depend on expanding demand. It is a vicious circle, which can be epitomized in the following points.

(1) In a highly concentrated economy, there is a bias in favor of labor-saving investment.

(2) In oligopolistic and monopolistic industries, investment that increases the demand for labor depends on a rise in effective demand; this is not so where competition prevails. The inducement to such investment, which could derive from a widespread reduction of prices, and especially of factor prices, works within narrow limits because the competitive mechanism works within narrow limits.

(3) Wage increases do not solve the problem; at best, they mitigate it. Looking at the problem in static terms, a wage reduction might seem advisable, in line with Wicksell's view. But such a reduction would only aggravate the dynamic problem: the problem of unemployment due to a *continuous* process of mechanization, in which labor is displaced even by the new machines bought out of depreciation funds to replace those gradually wearing out.

(4) Unless demand expands rapidly enough, oligopolistic or monopolistic profits may yield more disposable funds than are required for self-financing, and these may be kept in liquid form or employed "unproductively"; in these circumstances, a part of personal savings may also be hoarded.

In summary, in a highly concentrated economy the forces generating unemployment tend to be stronger than those absorbing it. There seems to be no *spontaneous* mechanism tending, even in an intermittent (cyclical) manner, to equalize the two sets of forces. The situation looks rather like Keynes's unemployment equilibrium, but in this case the unemployment is not static but dynamic.

Keynes has offered various prescriptions for breaking out of the vicious circle: a reduction in the rate of interest; a redistributive tax policy apt to increase the propensity to consume; a policy of massive public expenditure, productive and unproductive; and the "social control of investment." A reduction in the rate of interest is now generally recognized to have little effect. Progressive taxation of higher personal incomes and corporate profits may be helpful, though of course only up to a "critical point" beyond which it defeats its own purpose and, naturally, only if the government spends the money which would otherwise have been hoarded or employed in such a manner as not to raise demand. A redistributive tax policy may attenuate, though not solve, the problem, just as trade-union action may be effective up to a point through pushing up wages relatively more than profits.

Public expenditure will be discussed at some length in the next chapter (where we shall also, briefly and to some extent implicitly, touch upon the "social control of investment"). Public expenditure seems to hold out the best promise for mitigating the effective-demand problem. At any rate, this is true in a closed economy; in an open economy, foreign demand, or exports, must also be considered. In reality, of course, all economies are "open"; the question is how important exports are in relation to gross national product. If exports account for a large proportion of gross national product, as they do, say, in Great Britain and West Germany, the expansion or contraction of exports may assume considerable relevance for the problem under discussion; if they are relatively small, as in the United States, export changes have little effect, and the nub of the question remains public expenditure.

XI

Stagnation and Public Spending

Keynes's short-period analysis of unemployment lends itself easily to adaptation to the long period, and the link is provided precisely by the concept of unemployment equilibrium.[1] Among the followers of Keynes who made the attempt, Alvin Hansen stands out,[2] but he seems to have tackled only part of the logical difficulties inherent in the application to the long period of a conceptual apparatus worked out for the short period. In this respect Hansen departs from Keynes only in a few, and relatively unimportant, points. For our purposes, the details of Hansen's analysis are not relevant. We shall therefore merely outline it in extremely simplified terms.

Hansen's theory

According to Hansen, a very advanced economy, such as the United States's, possesses an enormous capacity to save. Saving is largely institutional and as such almost automatic; it depends essentially on the level of income and is fairly unresponsive to changes in the rate of interest. If savings are wholly invested, there will be full or nearly full employment; if investment opportunities are lacking, there will be more or less pronounced unemployment, which will tend to become chronic. There can be no presumption that *private* investment will be sufficient, for two major reasons: (1) in our century the possibilities of territorial

---

[1] Keynes himself more than once made remarks implying such an extension of his analysis. See *The General Theory of Employment, Interest and Money,* pp. 30, 33, 249.

[2] See, in particular, A. H. Hansen, *Full Recovery or Stagnation?* esp. chap. 1. In the introduction (p. 7), Hansen states explicitly: "This book deals not only with the problem of cyclical fluctuations but also with the larger problem of full employment of resources from the long-run point of view."

STAGNATION AND PUBLIC SPENDING

expansion are all but exhausted; (2) population growth in the
United States and other developed countries has a tendency to
slow down gradually. Hansen somewhat doubtfully mentions a
third reason. He asks himself

whether inventions and innovations are not likely in the future to be
less capital-using than in the nineteenth century. In contrast, while we
were in process of changing over from a direct [artisan] method of production to an elaborate capitalistic technique, as in the last century, innovations perforce had to be capital-using in character (p. 315).

The first reason (territorial expansion) has been convincingly
criticized by Schumpeter.[3] The second (population growth) we
have already mentioned in Chapter 10. The third reason is interesting: in substance, it concerns the question of replacement
investment. However, if our preceding analysis is correct, the fact
that this type of investment tends to become more frequent is
due, or could be due, not to the changeover to which Hansen
alludes (and which, after all, occurred a long time ago in the
more advanced countries) but to the spreading of oligopolistic
and monopolistic formations. Hansen poses the problem with
reference to the total outlet which savings can find in investment.
He fails to notice that the problem connected with this type of
investment lies not so much in its being less extensive than other
investments; the problem is that it generates unemployment.
Moreover, investment of this type implies changes in the state of
technology: Hansen, as we have noted, follows Keynes but does
not explain how the Keynesian analysis, which assumes constant
technology, can be reconciled with his own third reason, which
precludes such an assumption.

As a remedy for the stagnation tendency of private investment,
Hansen attaches particular weight to the third of the remedies
Keynes prescribes: an increase in public expenditure.[4] He feels
that such an increase may provide an alternative to economic
stagnation, which is a long-run tendency. Nevertheless, Hansen,

---

[3] *Business Cycles*, p. 1034; *Capitalism, Socialism, and Democracy*, pp. 109–10,
117.
[4] See Federico Caffè, "La teoria della 'maturità economica' e la funzione degli
investimenti pubblici," in *Studi keynesiani*, G. U. Papi, ed. (Milan, 1953), pp.
230–65.

like Keynes, relies heavily on an analytical tool fashioned to examine only the short-run effects of public expenditure on employment: the multiplier.

The multiplier and the degree of industrialization

The original maker of this analytical tool, R. F. Kahn, was careful to stress the assumptions on which it rests.[5] There are three of them: (1) high elasticity of supply of consumer goods — an increase in demand is translated into an almost proportional increase in the supply of goods and the price increase is negligible; (2) high elasticity of supply of labor — again, an increase in demand raises employment almost proportionately, with negligible wage increases; and (3) unchanging technology. Furthermore, Kahn neglects the question of the productivity of public expenditure. In considering its short-run effects, he says, it does not matter whether the expenditure is productive or unproductive.

According to Kahn, the first two assumptions are justified during depression. Speaking of the first, he says:

at times of intense depression, when nearly all industries have at their disposal a large surplus of unused plant and labour, the supply curve is likely to be very elastic. The amount of secondary employment is then large and the rise in prices is small (p. 182).

The reference to unused plant clearly indicates that Kahn has in mind industrial firms. He is correct in this because the multiplier, insofar as it works, works essentially in industry, not in agriculture.

What corresponds in agriculture to industrial plant is land. However, barring exceptional cases, farmers do not reduce the cultivated area during a depression; on the contrary, they sometimes increase it — understandably enough, since competition prevails and fixed costs are very high. Prices fall appreciably and large unsold stocks accumulate. As long as stocks are higher than normal, an increase in effective demand has no effect on production and employment.[6] Once stocks have returned to normal,

[5] "The Relation of Home Investment to Employment," *Economic Journal*, June 1931, pp. 173–98.

[6] Keynes himself points this out in general terms: "I should attribute the slow rate of recovery from a slump, after the turning-point has been reached, mainly

production will tend to expand but, in the short run, at rising costs and hence at rising prices.[7] This means that the multiplier can apply only to highly industrialized societies. In predominantly agricultural economies, where the standard of living is relatively low and expenditure on food occupies an important place in family budgets, the multiplier, while possibly having stimulating effects on the industrial sector, will tend to exhaust itself quickly in an inflationary process. The propensity to consume which is relevant to the multiplier is the propensity to consume industrial products.

In a relatively backward economy, where agriculture is the principal economic activity, the policy of expanding public expenditure is bound to have much less success in stimulating production and employment, and much greater chances of giving rise, from the outset, to strong inflationary pressures, if not to full-fledged inflation. Naturally, this conclusion applies only to public expenditure which is either unproductive or productive only in the long period. It does not apply to what is properly called productive public expenditure, or public investment in the strict sense of the word.

The productivity of public expenditure

The conclusion indicated above corresponds to the widely held opinion that in not highly industrialized economies unemployment does not respond to the Keynesian prescriptions. With reference to backward economies, the expression "structural unemployment" has become current, to mark the difference from cyclical and chronic unemployment, which derive from deficiency of demand due to excess saving and are a feature of highly industrialized economies. But, from an analytical point of view, the distinction between these kinds of unemployment is perhaps less sharp than one might think.

---

to the deflationary effect of the reduction of redundant stocks to a normal level" (*General Theory*, p. 331).

[7] The increase in demand and prices may stimulate the use of fertilizers and agricultural machines; but this implies changes in the technical coefficients, and these are excluded in the multiplier theory. In any case, these changes do not raise employment but, at least insofar as mechanization increases, tend to reduce it.

174 EFFECTIVE DEMAND AND ECONOMIC STAGNATION

One of the most interesting attempts at explaining structural unemployment in underdeveloped countries was made by a group of economists, including Rosenstein-Rodan, who connected it with technological discontinuities. These discontinuities give rise to a relative surplus of labor largely independent of wages.

If it is correct, as we have tried to argue, that the process of concentration accentuates technological discontinuities and thereby generates oligopolistic formations, which in turn weaken the forces tending to reabsorb the workers displaced by new machines, then there is, in the last analysis, no substantial difference between structural unemployment in underdeveloped countries and the chronic unemployment which was a feature of the interwar period and which may well occur in advanced economies. The root of the evil, in both cases, would be the technological discontinuities. However, the technological gap between the artisan and the modern firm is much greater than that between different techniques in an already advanced industry. Moreover, in an advanced economy an increase in demand may, at least within certain limits and for a certain time, stimulate various types of investment originating in a broad and diffused entrepreneurial class that is always on the lookout for favorable market developments to exploit. But in an underdeveloped country the entrepreneurial class is minute; in the very limited industrial sector monopolistic formations are the rule rather than oligopolistic ones; and external stimuli are incomparably less effective than in advanced economies.

For these reasons, as well as for those indicated in the preceding discussion of the relationship between the multiplier and the degree of industrialization, it would seem that the chronic unemployment of highly industrialized economies can be cured, at least for a time, with Keynesian remedies; but the structural unemployment of underdeveloped countries does not respond to the treatment because an increase in (unproductive) public expenditure comes to grief through decreasing agricultural returns and immediately generates inflationary pressures. However, even if Keynes's prescriptions are more likely to succeed in an advanced economy, can they represent a satisfactory (that is, stable) solution to the problem of stagnation tendencies in employment?

As Hansen correctly observed, a temporary increase in public expenditure might be effective if the problem consisted exclusively of cyclical unemployment; but it cannot resolve the problem of stagnation, granted that such a problem exists.[8] He stressed the obvious, but often neglected, fact that additional public investment stimulates production and alleviates unemployment only as long as the expenditure lasts; when it is interrupted, both primary and secondary employment disappear.[9] Consequently, Hansen became an advocate of uninterrupted growth in public expenditure as the only alternative to stagnation (which, to him, means stagnation in private investment).[10] But here we must ask whether it is really possible to neglect the question of the productivity of public expenditure once we leave the short for the long period.

In the first place, public expenditure can be covered not only by tax revenues and loans but also by new money created *ad hoc;* if so covered, it generates inflationary pressures which may be tolerable in the short run but which eventually lead to mounting difficulties of a kind too well known to require comment. To the extent that public expenditure is covered by taxes and loans (loans ultimately again involve taxation to cover the interest charges), it can expand without creating difficulties, as long as taxation increases at a rate not higher than the rate of increase of national income. If the two rates are equal, the proportion of national income absorbed by taxation remains constant. If taxation increases faster than national income, the tax burden grows; but it cannot grow indefinitely — from a certain point on, a critical limit or, better, a critical zone is reached beyond which taxation causes growing frictions.

[8] *Full Recovery or Stagnation?* pp. 294–302.
[9] See also J. M. Clark's valuable study, "An Appraisal of the Workability of Compensatory Devices," *American Economic Review,* Supplement, March 1939; reprinted in *Readings in Business Cycle Theory,* G. Haberler, ed. (Philadelphia, 1944), pp. 291–310.
[10] A. H. Hansen, "Some Notes on Terborgh's 'The Bogey of Economic Maturity,' " *Review of Economic Statistics,* no. 1 (1946); see also Caffè, "La teoria della maturità economica," p. 256.

Productive public expenditures have two kinds of positive effect on national income, one direct and one indirect. The direct effect derives simply from their being productive, and the indirect effect, which we have discussed, is that they generate an expansion of demand and thereby stimulate investment by private firms. Unproductive public expenditure has only the second effect, which does not outlast the expenditure itself. If the share of the unproductive in total public expenditure is large and growing, the rate of increase in public expenditure is likely to exceed the rate of increase in national income, and this cannot go on indefinitely.

Keynes, like Kahn, concerned himself primarily with the short period, and with reference to this he maintained that public expenditures could be useful in stimulating production and employment regardless of whether they were productive or unproductive. The famous and witty examples of pyramid building and of banknotes first buried and then dug up again illustrate the argument. But Keynes himself repeatedly declared his predilection for productive investment, which, apart from its transient stimulating effect, durably increases production and employment.

Pyramid-building, earthquakes, even wars may serve to increase wealth, if the education of our statesmen on the principles of the classical economics stands in the way of anything better. . . . It would, indeed, be more sensible to build houses and the like; but if there are political and practical difficulties in the way of this, the above would be better than nothing.[11]

The problem is more complex and the difficulties which Keynes mentions much more serious than he admits. First of all, the expansion of public expenditure involves more than purely technical or financial questions. Any increase in traditional public expenditure (which is not directly productive) is subject to institutional and organizational limitations that cannot easily be bypassed or changed, at any rate in the short run.[12] Over time, these limitations can, of course, be modified or pushed further out, but only at the cost of far-reaching institutional transforma-

[11] *General Theory*, p. 129.
[12] Even the Roosevelt administration, for all its immediate sympathy with Keynesian ideas and prescriptions, stepped very carefully — too carefully, in Keynes's own view — when it came to increasing public expenditure.

tions. In the case of directly productive public expenditure, or public investment properly speaking, the difficulties are still greater. The government here trespasses on the field of private enterprise and has to face resistance far beyond the circle of interests directly affected; it is a problem of the widest political implications. On the other hand, the difficulties and resistance are much less in the case of unproductive public expenditure, which generally does not disturb vested interests, or even favors them, and which in any event does not raise any serious organizational or political problems. Examples of peacetime expenditure of this kind are public works designed wholly or mainly to provide work for the unemployed; in times of war, or cold war, military expenditure falls into this category. But if one order of problems recedes in this case, another comes forward. If public expenditure of this kind is systematically expanded for any length of time, it generates inflationary pressures or indeed inflation, and in an economy with a high degree of industrial concentration inflation is a singularly intractable problem. Monetary policy loses much of its efficacy when many prices and wages, especially in key branches of production, are no longer the result of the impersonal play of demand and supply but are "administered" by companies and trade unions. There has been some talk of making wage and price administrators subject to certain controls, but any move in this direction would obviously encounter the strongest obstacles, particularly of an ideological and political nature.

Stagnation and public expenditure in the American economy

The public-spending problem poses itself at once in terms of economic policy, especially in periods of recession. But from the point of view of theory, it is one particular aspect of the problem of stagnation. William Fellner expresses it precisely in those terms:

Are we living in genuine prosperity, the fruits of which we are forced partly to sacrifice in the interest of national security, or are we living in a period of stagnation which is merely covered up by the international tension and by the consequent military and foreign aid expenditures?

It is true, of course, that our military and foreign aid expenditures are mainly tax-financed and that a hypothetical American economy with much lower government spending would also be an economy with a much lower tax burden. But this, in itself, does not answer the question. Tax reductions would but partly become expressed in increased consumption; in part they would be reflected in additional savings.[18] The question of whether a tendency toward genuine prosperity could be expected without high military expenditure or other expenditure of equivalent size calls for a discussion of the time rate of investment in a progressive economy.[14]

Let us briefly consider the basic elements of the problem, with particular reference to the United States, and in so doing let us recall some of the points discussed earlier.

Given the rise in productivity, employment can remain stable if national income grows at an annual rate of roughly 3 percent. Given the increase in the supply of labor as a result of population growth, unemployment can remain stable if national income rises by at least another 1 percent. Altogether, national income must grow by more than 4 percent anually.

This is exactly what happened, on the average, in the postwar period (1946–59). Gross national product grew by about $20 billion a year and, by 1959, had reached about $479 billion, distributed as follows: consumption, 310; private investment, 71 (new construction, 40.5, producers' durable equipment, 25.5, and inventory increases, 5); government purchases of goods and services, 98.

The average annual increment in gross national product ($20 billion) owed $12 billion to consumption, 3 to private investment, and 5 to public purchases. Because this increment was close enough to the "necessary" annual rate of increase of about 4 percent, unemployment had no marked tendency to rise, although it fluctuated around an average level of more than 3 million, which is by no means negligible and certainly more than what may be considered the level of frictional unemployment. Naturally, the various parts of the economy did not all grow at the same rate. Agricultural income rose only a little, and the higher productivity

[18] It should furthermore be kept in mind that, indirectly, part of the taxable income is actually generated by public expenditure, as R. F. Kahn notes in his paper on the multiplier. A contraction of public expenditure would, therefore, not set free individual incomes of equal amount; it would cause some of them to disappear. — P. S. L.

[14] "Full Use or Underutilization of Resources: Appraisal of Long-run Factors other than Defense," *American Economic Review*, May 1954, p. 422.

of farming was translated into a corresponding net decrease in the active farm population; in industry and in the tertiary sector, the growth of income exceeded the rise in productivity.

In 1959 the structure of employment in the United States was as follows. Of a total of about 60 million employed, almost 10 percent worked in agriculture, 39 percent in industry, and 34 percent in services, including finance and trade but excluding government and the armed forces. The government accounted for 13 percent and the military for 4 percent. Every year an average of 600–700,000 persons enter the labor market, subject to cyclical variations (there are more new entrants during prosperity, fewer in depression).

Farming not only absorbs no new labor but on the average releases some 200–300,000 persons each year. Industry absorbs about as many. More than 400,000 people go into services (excluding government and military) each year, and about 200,000 enter government service. Thus services absorb most of the additional labor supply.

In general terms, the mechanism works in the following way. Productivity increments are distributed largely through rising incomes rather than through falling prices. Rising incomes mean rising profits, which imply higher investable funds and, to a lesser extent, higher consumer expenditure; they also mean rising wages and salaries, which are translated mainly into higher consumer demand and, to a lesser extent, higher saving. Among consumer goods, services occupy an increasingly important place. Productivity increments are not fully translated into increments in consumer demand, since considerable portions of profits and small portions of wages and salaries are almost automatically saved. This is the origin of the problem of the adequacy of investment opportunities, and this is where the vicious circle may start. Keynes was right: there is a problem in the propensity to save — though the problem rests not on psychological motives but on well-defined objective factors. These are, first, the determinants of investment decisions, especially in highly concentrated industries, and, second, the determinants of personal saving. There is also a problem of investment opportunities, though, again, not so much in Hansen's terms of the danger of exhausted investment opportunities but for reasons connected with outlets in highly concentrated industries.

If the system were left to itself, it would in the long run tend to grow too slowly to ensure full employment; on the contrary, unemployment would tend to increase. There is an organic need for supplementary demand, which in the long period stems from the government's spending, financed by loans, additional money, and tax revenue (especially progressive taxes on higher incomes, that is to say, funds which, if not taxed away, would in part have been used in ways other than to increase productive capacity and thereby national income and employment). Indirectly, the growth of public expenditure stimulates investment in the private sector. Growth of public expenditure thus holds a key position in the development of the economic system and has superseded private investment as the principal dynamic element.

Consider again the American economy during the period 1946–59. The ascendency of public expenditure over private investment stands out: total private investment was in the neighborhood of $70 billion; public purchases of goods and services ran to about $100 billion. During the period in question the annual increment of private investment was, on the average, $3 billion (more than $2 billion for new construction and about $1 billion for plant and machinery), while public purchases rose, on the average, by some $5 billion a year. Actually, public expenditure as such grew even more than public purchases, which exclude transfer payments. The effects of the latter, of course, are not exhausted by a mere redistribution of spending; if, as is likely, a certain amount of purchasing power is withdrawn from groups with a lower propensity to consume and directed to groups with a higher propensity to consume, transfer payments raise national income, though it is hard to say by how much. The overall annual increment of public expenditure during the period under consideration was about $6 billion.

In the course of the twentieth century, United States public expenditure rose not only in absolute terms but also in relation to gross national product (see the accompanying table). If there is any truth in the argument of this book, the increase was not,

United States public expenditure, 1903-59
(in billions of current dollars)

Year	Public expenditure Total	By federal government	Gross national product	Ratio of public expenditure to gross national product (%)
1903	1.7	0.5	23[a]	7.4
1913	3.1	0.7	40[a]	7.7
1929	10.4	3.3	99[a]	10.5
1939	16.8	9.0	91	18.4
1949	59.8	40.1	258	23.1
1959	125.0[b]	80.0[c]	479	26.0

[a] Gross national product for 1903 is an estimate; strictly speaking, neither this figure nor those for 1913 and 1929 is comparable with the more recent ones, since the method of calculation was somewhat different. But for our purposes we need only the order of magnitude of GNP during the various years, and to this end the comparison seems legitimate (see The Economic Almanac, p. 509n).

[b] Estimated.

[c] The principal items of federal expenditure are: military expenditure, 46.1; veterans' benefits, 4.9; interest on public debt, 8.3; foreign economic aid, 2.0.

Sources: S. Fabricant, The Trend of Government Activity in the United States since 1900 (New York, 1952), p. 27; The Economic Almanac 1953-54, National Industrial Conference Board (New York, 1954), pp. 486, 509, 524; U. S. Department of Commerce, Survey of Current Business, July 1959, April 1960.

and is not, due to accidental factors and exogenous circumstances; it is a necessary result of the progressive structural transformation of the economic system, and of industry in particular. In the last analysis, the phenomenon is connected with the process of industrial concentration.

American public expenditure in the postwar period

With particular reference to the postwar period in the United States, there can be no doubt that the increase in public expenditure played a significant part in the economy's expansion. Most of the increase went into military expenditure, which in turn was a response to international tension. In his textbook on economics, Paul Samuelson writes:

The six years since 1945 have proved to be quite the reverse of any gloomy expectations concerning the stagnation of a mature economy. And as long as the present tense international situation prevails, there seems to be small reason to fear that there will be too little dollar spending in the U.S. It is ironical that the Russians accept it as an inevitable fact that the postwar capitalistic system must experience a tremendous crisis and collapse. Yet every military move they make has the quite opposite effect of ensuring that the capitalist countries will pursue such expensive military expenditures as to make any depression impossible![15]

Should world tension be substantially lessened, the problem which Hansen raised a few years ago would reappear in pressing terms:

Let us assume, however, that we *do* have a drastic cut in military expenditures. In that event, two views have already been expressed rather forcibly before the country. One is what I would call, perhaps not quite accurately, the government point of view; at least a good many government officials have expressed this point of view. The other is what I would call, again perhaps not quite accurately, the business point of view; at least I find it continually expressed in the financial press. The government point of view is optimistic and the business point of view pessimistic about the postwar readjustment.

The government point of view emphasizes the cushioning effect of many New Deal reforms — the social security program, the farm program, the banking reforms, reforms with respect to the issuing of securities, home financing, and all the rest. These things put a cushion under any possible recession. A decline of $20 billion is now contemplated in the defense program after 1954. What is $20 billion, we are asked, in comparison with the decline of something like $120 billion, in terms of 1951 prices, that actually occurred after the war? We got along quite well then, so why not now? That view has been expressed in certain government quarters, and I call it the optimistic point of view.

On the other side, the pessimistic view suggests that the postwar experience is not now likely to be repeated. This is true, it is said, because in 1945 we had not had any capital formation to speak of for four years. We had built virtually no houses except in the defense areas, we had not built any automobiles for several years, we had a tremendous backlog of demand to meet for all sorts of things. In 1954 there is no prospect that there will be any such backlog. Consequently, the analogy is not thought to be adequate, and the question is raised whether there might be a considerable decline in the offing.[16]

---

[15] *Economics: An Introductory Analysis* (New York, 1951), p. 406. See also G. H. Hildebrand and N. V. Breckner, *The Impacts of National Security Expenditure upon the Stability and Growth of the American Economy,* Joint Economic Committee, Subcommittee on Fiscal Policy, 85th Congress, 1st Session, November 5, 1957 (Washington, 1958), pp. 523–41.

[16] A. H. Hansen, "Savings in the Expanding United States Economy: The Record of the Forties and the Prospects for the Fifties," in *Savings in the*

We may add that after the war the United States witnessed the withdrawal from the labor market and the return to domestic activities of something like 4 million women, who in many civilian occupations had replaced the servicemen.[17] This experience, too, is not likely to be repeated.

The problem does exist and it is a serious one. Many economists agree that this is so, but a good many more either ignore the problem or deny its existence by means of arguments which, at first sight, appear to be both simple and strong.

These arguments run as follows. Public expenditure has obviously become a key factor in today's economy and a sudden contraction in public, and especially military, spending would administer too rude a shock to a system which has taken to the habit-forming poison of gigantic public expenditure and enormous government orders. No physician would advise, say, a drug addict to give up his vice all at once; but he may advise him to cut down the doses gradually. Similarly, the economist may advise a gradual reduction in government spending; there will then be no shock and the economic system will pick up spontaneously.

This, of course, is precisely the point. This writer believes that by and large such an argument could stand up a few decades ago, but that today, in an economy as highly industrialized and concentrated as the American, the system can be saved from stagnation and growing unemployment only by continuously high and, indeed, growing public expenditure.

Even among those economists who do recognize the existence of the problem, there are many who think that it will be relatively

---

Modern Economy: A Symposium, ed. W. W. Heller, F. M. Boddy, and C. L. Nelson (Minneapolis, 1953), pp. 53–4. (Copyright 1953 by the University of Minnesota.)

On postwar capital formation, see M. Sapir, "Review of Economic Forecasts for the Transition Period," in *Studies in Income and Wealth*, p. 323; C. A. Blyth, "The United States Cycle in Private Fixed Investment, 1946–1950," *Review of Economics and Statistics*, no. 1 (1956), p. 48.

On postwar backlog of demand, see Sapir, pp. 322–9; W. S. Woytinsky, "Relationship Between Consumers' Expenditures, Savings, and Disposable Incomes," *Review of Economics and Statistics*, no. 1 (1946), and "What was Wrong in Forecasts of Postwar Depression?" *Journal of Political Economy*, no. 2 (1947).

[17] *The Economic Almanac 1958*, National Industrial Conference Board (New York, 1959), p. 345.

easy to solve. Hansen himself, though with reservations, is of this opinion. The argument is that the negative effects of a drastic reduction in military expenditure — Hansen's $20 billion — can be offset by a combination of tax reduction and increased non-military public expenditure. In actual fact the problem is anything but easy to solve.

A tax reduction would cause only a less than proportional increase in the demand for goods produced by private firms, since consumers and, even more so, firms tend to save part of their income; the resulting saving could be invested only if there were investment opportunities, and these would definitely be reduced if public expenditure were curtailed.[18] The tax reduction would have to be accompanied by a budget deficit sufficient to offset the increased saving — that is, the tax reduction would have to be larger than the reduction in expenditure. But, quite apart from the problems of readjustment (demand for certain goods would fall, demand for others would rise), there is the serious difficulty that the government is always reluctant to cut taxes because, once cut, it is politically difficult to raise them again.

On the other hand, there is a growing consensus of opinion among economists that there is much to be said for increasing nonmilitary public expenditure under such important headings as education, scientific research for civilian purposes, hospitals, and so on. The most rational way out would seem to be a substantial and systematic increase in expenditures of this kind. But what commends itself as rational to the economist is not necessarily easy to carry out. Any program of large-scale expansion in productive public expenditure comes up against very serious political and organizational obstacles to which economists so far have not given enough attention. If, therefore, we arrive at conclusions rather like Keynes's, we reach them by a different road, or by a different analysis, which brings to light considerable differences in the practical problems involved. It is hard to exaggerate the extent of the political and social transformations implied by the solution of these problems.

They can be no more than touched upon here. As a first approach, one might well pass under critical review each of the cate-

[18] See also p. 178 n. 13.

gories of civilian public expenditure which might possibly be expanded. This review may, perhaps, uncover some of the obstacles to which I have alluded. Let me give one or two examples. We have already considered the barriers which stand in the way of directly productive public investment in any area in which private enterprise exists; we have also seen that it is not easy to expand traditional public expenditure quickly or to any sizable extent beyond the usual rate of growth. These difficulties are especially pronounced in the case of expenditure by the individual states, where administrative and financial organization impose strict limits. A massive increase in educational expenditure would raise the problem of the autonomy of universities and private institutions, together with the general problems of reorganization, which would, in any case, require considerable time. A massive increase in aid to underdeveloped countries would imply a radical change in foreign policy, such as is inconceivable without an equally radical change in domestic policy. Public health programs or extensive public investment for slum clearance and new housing are obviously bound to encounter political resistance. Then there are the well-known difficulties of budget approval. At times of international tension, Congress may readily enough approve big defense expenditures, while scrutinizing all other items with a strict eye to economy. This applies particularly to large-scale aid to underdeveloped countries, which lacks the support of powerful lobbies.

Let me make my meaning quite clear. I would not subscribe to the view — which, incidentally, has very few adherents among economists — that the American economy could not continue to expand and keep unemployment relatively low without massive defense expenditure. I do suggest, however, that if a considerable increase in unemployment is to be avoided, any substantial reduction in defense expenditure must be associated with an at least equal, and therefore very large, increase in other public expenditure; and it is to be feared that such an increase, far from raising mere technical or financial questions, would raise serious problems of a kind that could not be resolved without far-reaching organizational transformations and profound political change.

The policy of burying one's head in the sand has never helped anyone. The first step in the solution of a difficult problem is to recognize it clearly, and I believe that it is the duty of economists to help clarify the terms in which the problem poses itself.

Conclusion

We have seen that in a modern economy there exists a problem of the propensity to save, though it is not based on psychological motives, and that there exists also a problem of investment opportunities, not in terms of their exhaustion but in terms of the determinants of the investment decisions of large firms and of outlets in highly concentrated industries. The problems, therefore, pose themselves in much the same terms as Keynes and Hansen indicated. Demand is an essential element in our analysis, as it is in theirs, but for different reasons; these are already to be found, in embryonic form, in Chapter 30 of Ricardo's *Principles*.

The problem of the market form, which concerns individual firms, and the problem of effective demand, which concerns the economy as a whole, have always been discussed separately. The two questions have been treated by two different methods of analysis: microeconomic analysis in the neoclassical theory and macroeconomic analysis in Keynesian theory. The neoclassical theory of market forms has found severe critics in Sraffa and his successors, but its analytical instruments and quite a few of its assumptions have survived the reappraisal. What matters more is that the treatment of market forms is still set in the framework of partial equilibrium, save for a few notable exceptions such as the work of Kalecki and, in some important respects, that of Sweezy, Baran, and Robinson. Some have gone so far as to state that, contrary to neoclassical assumptions, we live in a "world of monopolies"; but it is not at all clear what the consequences of the progressive spreading of monopolistic or, more precisely, oligopolistic formations are for the tendencies of such aggregates as employment and national income. Many economists, while recognizing the diffusion of oligopolistic formations, regard them as having no effect on the trends of these economic aggregates. Keynes held to the assumption of perfect competition everywhere except in the labor market, and in any event he set the example of attributing little consequence to market forms, which seemed to him irrelevant for the purposes of his macroeconomic analysis. This is one of the reasons why micro- and macroeconomic analysis developed side by side independently rather than complementarily. Yet integration of the two types of analysis seems both feasible and desirable. In particular, it seems that the psychological assumptions, which are a weak point in Keynesian theory, may conveniently be replaced by objective assumptions. Such integration would surely be highly fruitful for the further progress of economic theory.

APPENDIX

WORKS CITED

INDEX

Appendix: Numerical Values
of Gini's Concentration Ratio
for United States Industry

I

(1) *Establishments classified according to the number of workers (manufacturing industry)*

1909	0.48	1921	0.52
1914	0.51	1923	0.53
1919	0.57	1947	0.59

The underlying statistics refer to industrial establishments with an output of not less a value than $5,000.

For the years 1909, 1914, 1919, 1921, and 1923 the size classes are: 0–5 workers, 6–50, 51–250, 251–1000, and more than 1000. For 1947 the size classes are 1–4, 5–49, 50–249, 250–999, and 1000 and over. This change in classification may raise some doubts as to whether the 1947 index is comparable with the others. But the change is small and, if it caused any appreciable shift in the number of establishments, it can only have been in the lowest class. It is quite possible that if in 1947 the size class had been not 1–4, but 0–5 as in the earlier years, it would have contained more, and perhaps many more, establishments. But even then it is highly unlikely that one single size class, however large, should make a decisive difference in the general index. To be on the safe side, I also calculated the indices for the earliest and latest years without the lowest class, and the indices still have a clear upward tendency:

(2)	1909	0.41
	1947	0.55

For 1951 I was able to find figures for only three size classes comparable with 1947: 1–249, 250–999, 1000 and over. The two indices are:

(3)	1947	0.447
	1951	0.466

Sources for the calculation of the above indices are: 1909 and 1914 — *Abstract of the Census of Manufactures,* 1914, pp. 390–1; 1919 — *Statistical Abstract,* 1922, p. 197; 1921 and 1923 — *Statistical Abstract,* 1924, p. 724; 1947 and 1951 — *The Economic Almanac 1953–54,* National Industrial Conference Board (New York, 1954), p. 249.

II

(1) *Establishments classified according to value of output (manufacturing industry)*

Four size classes, in thousands of dollars: 5–20, 20–100, 100–1000, 1000 and more

1904	0.625
1939	0.793

(2) *Establishments classified according to value added (manufacturing industry)*

1904	0.569
1939	0.764

These indices are much less reliable than the preceding ones, because a rising price level induces a change in the distribution of establishments which has nothing to do with the process of concentration. However, between the two years in question prices rose only to the relatively modest extent of 30 percent; the years following the Second World War were deliberately left out because of the much more violent price rises which would have made the comparison extremely doubtful.

The sources are the same as those indicated above.

III

(1) *Corporations classified by assets (manufacturing industry)*

Nine size classes, in millions of dollars: less than 50, 50–99, 100–249, 250–499, 500–999, 1000–4999, 5000–9999, 10,000–49,999, 50,-000 and more

1933	0.769	1945	0.800
1938	0.751	1946	0.765
1939	0.755	1947	0.776
1944	0.799	1948	0.810

Here we have the same difficulty of changing money values; but the first three years are reasonably comparable among themselves, and so are the last five years.

These indices too, like the preceding ones, show a tendency to rise.

Sources: 1933 to 1947 — *The Economic Almanac,* pp. 281, 314; 1951

— *Statistics of Income for 1951*, U. S. Department of Commerce, Part II, p. 130.

(2) *Share of value added by manufacture accounted for by largest companies, 1947 and 1954*

	1947	1954
Largest 50 companies	17	23
Largest 100 companies	23	30
Largest 150 companies	27	34
Largest 200 companies	30	37

(Data taken from *Report of the Subcommittee on Antitrust and Monopoly*, U. S. Senate, 85th Congress, 1st Session, Washington, 1957, p. 11.)

IV

In trying to calculate indices for separate industries we come up against a twofold difficulty — namely, classification changes in industrial censuses and changes in the nature and quality of the goods. I have calculated a few indices for industries where there was little or no change in classification and whose products can be supposed to have undergone only relatively slight modifications.

Establishments classified according to number of workers, in five manufacturing industries

(1) Steel works and rolling mills

1914	0.65
1947	0.88

(2) Electrical machinery

1914	0.73
1947	0.77

(3) Petroleum refining

1914	0.78
1947	0.84

(4) Lumber and timber products
(1947 census: "Lumber and products")

1914	0.45
1947	0.33

(5) Shipbuilding, iron and steel
(1947 census: "Shipbuilding and repairing")

1914	0.77
1947	0.81

The size classes are as follows — 1914 census: 1-5, 6-20, 21-50, 51-100, 101-250, 251-500, 500-1000, more than 1000; 1947 census: the lowest class is 1-4, and all the others are down by one unit. We encounter the same difficulty as in section I, but this would not seem to impair the comparability of the indices.

Sources: 1914 — *Abstract of the Census of Manufactures*, pp. 410-21; 1947 — *Census of Manufactures, 1947, General Report*, I.

Note the deconcentration in the lumber industry, an exceptional case among those examined. Other figures, which will not be examined here, such as prices and productivity per man-hour, suggest that in this industry real costs tend to rise and that, at least so far, technical improvements in the main served only to compensate decreasing yields due to the scarcity of natural resources (forests) and probably also to the fact that high transport costs stand in the way of any large economies of scale. Not only did the degree of concentration diminish in this industry, but in more than thirty years the total number of establishments remained almost unchanged at high levels (26,000), and the number of small establishments decreased only slightly (from 23,000 to 20,000 in the "up-to-twenty" group).

This special case underscores, by contrast, the ultimate significance of the concentration process: increase of efficiency in production.

Works Cited

Adams, W. "The Steel Industry," in *The Structure of American Industry*, ed. W. Adams. New York, 2nd ed., 1954.

Adelman, M. A. "The Measurement of Industrial Concentration," *Review of Economics and Statistics*, no. 4 (1951).

"Administered Prices — Automobiles." *Report . . . of the Subcommittee on Antitrust and Monopoly*, U. S. Senate, 85th Congress, 1st Session, 1958.

Allen, R. G. D. "The Concept of Arc Elasticity of Demand," *Review of Economic Studies*, June 1934.

Andrews, P. W. S. *Manufacturing Business*. London, 1949.

Bain, J. S. *Barriers to New Competition*. Cambridge, Mass., 1956.

——— "Conditions of Entry and the Emergence of Monopoly," in *Monopoly and Competition and Their Regulation*, ed. E. H. Chamberlin. London, 1954.

——— "Economies of Scale, Concentration, and the Condition of Entry in Twenty Manufacturing Industries," *American Economic Review*, March, 1954.

——— "A Note on Pricing in Monopoly and Oligopoly," *American Economic Review*, March 1949.

——— "The Profit Rate as Measure of Monopoly Power," *Quarterly Journal of Economics*, February 1941.

Baumol, W. J. *Business Behavior, Value and Growth*. New York, 1959.

Blair, J. M. "Administered Prices: A Phenomenon in Search of a Theory," *American Economic Review*, May 1959.

Blyth, C. A. "The United States Cycle in Private Fixed Investment, 1946–1950," *Review of Economics and Statistics*, no. 1 (1956).

Bowman, M. J. "A Graphical Analysis of Personal Income Distribution in the United States," *American Economic Review*, September 1945. Reprinted in *Readings in the Theory of Income Distribution*, ed. W. Fellner and B. F. Haley. Philadelphia, 1946.

Breglia, A. "Cenni di teoria della politica economica," *Giornale degli economisti*, 1934. Reprinted in *Temi di economia e vita sociale*. Milan, 1942.

——— *L'economia dal punto di vista monetario*. Rome, 3rd ed., 1951.

——— "Profitti sterili e profitto fecondo," *Giornale degli economisti*, May 1953.

——— *Reddito sociale*. Rome, 1951.

Bresciani-Turroni, C. *Corso di economia politica.* Milan, 2nd ed., 1954.

Caffè, F. "La teoria della 'maturità economica' e la funzione degli investimenti pubblici," in *Studi keynesiani,* ed. G. U. Papi. Milan, 1953.

Chamberlin, E. H. "Full Cost and Monopolistic Competition," *Economic Journal,* June 1952.

—————— *The Theory of Monopolistic Competition.* Cambridge, Mass., 5th ed., 1947.

Clapham, J. H. *An Economic History of Modern England,* I — *The Early Railway Age;* III — *Machines and National Rivalries.* Cambridge, Eng., 1951.

Clark, C. *National Income and Outlay.* London, 1937.

Clark, J. M. "An Appraisal of the Workability of Compensatory Devices," *American Economic Review,* Supplement, March 1939.

—————— "Toward a Concept of Workable Competition," *American Economic Review,* June 1940.

"Concentration in American Industry." *Report . . . of the Subcommittee on Antitrust and Monopoly,* U. S. Senate, 85th Congress, 1st Session, 1957.

Copeland, M. A. "The Theory of Monopolistic Competition," *Journal of Political Economy,* no. 4 (1934).

Crum, W. L. *Corporate Size and Earning Power.* Cambridge, Mass., 1939.

Cyert, R. M., and J. C. March. "Organizational Factors in the Theory of Monopoly," *Quarterly Journal of Economics,* February 1956.

De Bodt, J. P. *La formation des prix: Analyse des rapports entre la théorie et la politique industrielle.* Brussels, 1956.

Douglas, P. *Real Wages in the United States, 1890–1926.* Boston, 1928.

Dunlop, J. T. "Price Inflexibility and the 'Degree of Monopoly,'" *Quarterly Journal of Economics,* August 1939.

Eckaus, R. S. "The Factor Proportions Problem in Underdeveloped Areas," *American Economic Review,* no. 4 (1955).

Einaudi, L. "Debiti," *Riforma sociale,* nos. 1–2 (1934). Reprinted in *Nuovi saggi.* Turin, 1937.

Ellis, H. S., ed. *A Survey of Contemporary Economics.* Philadelphia, 1948.

Evely, R., and I. M. D. Little. *Concentration in British Industry.* Cambridge, Eng., 1960.

Fabricant, S. *The Trend of Government Activity in the United States since 1900.* New York, 1952.

Fanno, M. *Lezioni di economia e di scienza bancaria.* Padua, 1937.

—————— *La teoria delle fluttuazioni economiche.* Turin, 1947.

Faulkner, H. U. *American Economic History.* New York, 6th ed., 1949.

Fellner, W. *Competition among the Few: Oligopoly and Similar Market Structures.* New York, 1949.

—————— "Full Use or Underutilization of Resources: Appraisal of Long-

Run Factors Other than Defense," *American Economic Review*, May 1954.

Fisher, I. Statement in *Proceedings of the National Conference on Trusts and Combinations, Chicago, October 1907*. National Civic Federation. New York, 1908.

Galbraith, J. K. "Market Structure and Stabilization Policy," *Review of Economics and Statistics*, no. 2 (1957).

—— "Monopoly and the Concentration of Economic Power," in *A Survey of Contemporary Economics*, ed. H. S. Ellis. Philadelphia, 1948.

—— "Monopoly Power and Price Rigidities," *Quarterly Journal of Economics*, May 1936.

Garbarino, J. W. "A Theory of Interindustry Wage Structure Variations," *Quarterly Journal of Economics*, May 1950.

Garcke, E., and J. M. Fells. *Factory Accounts: Their Principles and Practice*. New York, 6th ed., 1912.

Gini, C. "Sulla misura della concentrazione e della variabilità dei caratteri," *Atti del Reale Istituto Veneto di scienze, lettere ed arti*, LXXIII, part 2.

Gordon, R. A. "Short-Period Price Determination," *American Economic Review*, June 1948.

Haberler, G. *Prosperity and Depression*. Lake Success, 3rd ed., 1946.

Haberler, G., ed. *Readings in Business Cycle Theory*. Philadelphia, 1944.

Halcrow, H. C., ed. *Contemporary Readings in Agricultural Economics*. New York, 1955.

Hall, R. L., and C. J. Hitch. "Price Theory and Economic Behaviour," *Oxford Economic Papers*, 1939.

Hansen, A. H. *Full Recovery or Stagnation?* London, 1938.

—— *Monetary Theory and Fiscal Policy*. New York, 1949.

—— "Savings in the Expanding United States Economy: The Record of the Forties and the Prospects for the Fifties," in *Savings in the Modern Economy: A Symposium*, ed. W. W. Heller, F. M. Boddy, and C. L. Nelson. Minneapolis, 1953.

—— "Some Notes on Terborgh's 'The Bogey of Economic Maturity,' " *Review of Economic Statistics*, February 1946.

Harrod, R. F. *Economic Essays*. London, 1952.

—— "Imperfect Competition and the Trade Cycle," *Review of Economics and Statistics*, no. 2 (1936).

Heflebower, R. B. "Full Costs, Cost Changes, and Prices," in *Business Concentration and Price Policy*. National Bureau of Economic Research. Princeton, 1955.

Henderson, A. "The Theory of Duopoly," *Quarterly Journal of Economics*, November 1954.

Hicks, J. R. *A Contribution to the Theory of the Trade Cycle*. Oxford, 1950.

Hildebrand, G. H., and N. V. Breckner. *The Impact of National Security Expenditure upon the Stability and Growth of the American Economy.* Joint Economic Committee, 85th Congress, 1st Session. Washington, 1958.

Hines, H. H. "Effectiveness of 'Entry' by Already Established Firms," *Quarterly Journal of Economics,* February 1957.

Hise, van, C. R. *Concentration and Control.* New York, 1915.

Kahn, R. F. "The Relation of Home Investment to Employment," *Economic Journal,* June 1931.

Kaldor, N. "Alternative Theories of Distribution," *Review of Economic Studies,* no. 61 (1955–56).

────── "Market Imperfection and Excess Capacity," *Economica,* February 1935.

Kalecki, M. "The Determinants of Distribution of National Income," *Econometrica,* April 1938.

────── *Essays in the Theory of Economic Fluctuations.* London, 1938.

────── *Theory of Economic Dynamics.* New York, 1954.

Kaplan, A. D. H., J. B. Dirlam, and R. F. Lanzillotti. *Pricing in Big Business — A Case Approach.* Washington, 1958.

Keynes, J. M. *Essays in Persuasion.* London, 1931.

────── *The General Theory of Employment, Interest and Money.* London, 1936.

────── *A Treatise on Money.* 2 vols. New York, 1930.

Knight, W. R. "Agriculture," in *The Structure of American Industry,* ed. W. Adams. New York, 2nd ed., 1954.

Lange, O. *Price Flexibility and Employment.* Bloomington, 1944.

Lawrence, W. B. *Cost Accounting.* New York, 1954.

Layton, W. T., and G. Crowther. *An Introduction to the Study of Prices.* London, 1935.

Leak, H., and A. Maizels. "The Structure of British Industry," *Journal of the Royal Statistical Society,* 1945.

Leontief, W. "Elasticity of Demand Computed from Cost Data," *American Economic Review,* December 1940.

Lerner, A. P. "The Concept of Monopoly and the Measurement of Monopoly Power," *Review of Economic Studies,* June 1934. Reprinted in A. P. Lerner, *Essays in Economic Analysis.* London, 1953.

Levy, H. *Monopoly and Competition.* London, 1911.

────── *The New Industrial System.* London, 1936.

Liebling, H. I. "Financing Business in Recession and Expansion," *Survey of Current Business,* October 1958.

Lombardini, S. *Il monopolio nella teoria economica.* Milan, 1953.

Lynch, D. *The Concentration of Economic Power.* New York, 1946.

Machlup, F. *The Political Economy of Monopoly.* Baltimore, 1952.

Marshall, A. *Industry and Trade.* London, 3rd ed., 1923.

────── *Principles of Economics.* London, 8th ed., 1920.

Marx, K. *Das Kapital*. Dietz, Berlin, 1947–1951.
—— *Theorien über den Mehrwert*, II: *David Ricardo*. Dietz, Stuttgart, 1905.
Mason, E. S. *Economic Concentration and the Monopoly Problem*. Cambridge, Mass., 1957.
—— "Price Inflexibility," *Review of Economic Statistics*, no. 2 (1938).
Means, G. C. *Industrial Prices and Their Relative Inflexibility*. Senate Document No. 13, 74th Congress, 1st Session. Washington, 1935.
Mercillon, H. "Nouvelles orientations de la théorie de l'oligopole," *Revue d'économie politique*, no. 1 (1961).
Meyer, J. R., and E. Kuh. *The Investment Decision: An Empirical Study*. Cambridge, Mass., 1957.
Modigliani, F. "Fluctuations in the Saving-Income Ratio," in *Studies in Income and Wealth*, XI. National Bureau of Economic Research. New York, 1949.
—— "Liquidity Preference and the Theory of Interest and Money," *Econometrica*, 1944. Reprinted in *Readings in Monetary Theory*, ed. F. A. Lutz and L. W. Mints. Philadelphia, 1951.
—— "New Developments on the Oligopoly Front," *Journal of Political Economy*, no. 3 (1958).
Napoleoni, C. "Oligopolio," *Dizionario di economia politica*. Milan, 1956.
National Bureau of Economic Research. *Business Concentration and Price Policy*. Princeton, 1955.
—— *Cost Behavior and Price Policy*. New York, 1943.
National Industrial Conference Board. *The Economic Almanac 1953–54* and *1958*. New York, 1954 and 1959.
Neal, A. C. *Industrial Concentration and Price Inflexibility*. Washington, 1942.
Nelson, S., W. G. Keim, and E. S. Mason, *Price Behavior and Business Policies*. Temporary National Economic Committee Monograph No. 1 (1940).
Nickerson, C. B. *Cost Accounting*. New York, 1954.
Nutter, C. W. *The Extent of Enterprise Monopoly in the United States, 1899–1939*. Chicago, 1951.
Oxford Studies in the Price Mechanism, ed. T. Wilson and P. W. S. Andrews. Oxford, 1951.
Pantaleoni, M. "Di alcuni fenomeni di dinamica economica," *Scritti varii di economia*. Rome, 1910. Reprinted as "Some Phenomena of Economic Dynamics," trans. S. d'Amico, in *International Economic Papers*, 1955.
—— *Erotemi di economia*. Laterza, Bari, 1925.
Pareto, V. *Manuale di economia politica*. Milan, 1906.
Patinkin, D. "Price Flexibility and Full Employment," *American Economic Review*, 1948. Reprinted in *Readings in Monetary Theory*, ed. F. A. Lutz and L. W. Mints. Philadelphia, 1951.

200 WORKS CITED

Pigou, A. C. *Industrial Fluctuations.* London, 1929.
Ricardo. D. *Works and Correspondence,* ed. P. Sraffa. 10 vols. Cambridge, Eng., 1952. Vol. I: *Principles of Political Economy and Taxation.* Vol. IV: *Essay on Profits.*
Robinson, J. *The Accumulation of Capital.* London, 1956.
———— *The Economics of Imperfect Competition.* London, 1933.
Rosenbluth, G. "Measures of Concentration," in *Business Concentration and Price Policy.* National Bureau of Economic Research. Princeton, 1955.
Rosenman, S. I., ed. *The Public Papers and Addresses of Franklin D. Roosevelt,* 13 vols. New York, 1938–1950. Vol. VII: *The Continuing Struggle for Liberalism.*
Rosenstein-Rodan, P. "Rapporti fra fattori produttivi nell'economia italiana," *L'industria,* no. 4 (1954).
Ross, A. M., and W. Goldner. *Quarterly Journal of Economics,* May 1950.
Rothschild, K. W. "The Degree of Monopoly," *Economica,* February 1942.
Ruggles, R. "The Nature of Price Flexibility and the Determinants of Relative Price Changes in the Economy," in *Business Concentration and Price Policy.* National Bureau of Economic Research. Princeton, 1955.
Samuelson, P. *Economics: An Introductory Analysis.* New York, 1951.
Sapir, M. "Review of Economic Forecasts for the Transition Period," *Studies in Income and Wealth,* XI. National Bureau of Economic Research. New York, 1949.
Schneider, E. *Theorie der Produktion.* Vienna, 1934.
Schumpeter, J. A. *Business Cycles.* New York, 1939.
———— *Capitalism, Socialism, and Democracy.* New York, 1947.
———— *History of Economic Analysis.* London, 1954.
———— *Theory of Economic Development.* Cambridge, Mass., 1934.
Shubik, M. *Strategy and Market Structure: Competition, Oligopoly, and the Theory of Games.* New York, 1959.
Singer, H. W. "The Distribution of Gains between Investing and Borrowing Countries," *American Economic Review,* May 1950.
Smith, A. *Wealth of Nations,* ed. E. Cannan. London, 1904.
Sraffa, P. "The Laws of Returns under Competitive Conditions," *Economic Journal,* December 1926.
Staehle, H. "The Measurement of Statistical Cost Functions: An Appraisal of Some Recent Contributions," *American Economic Review,* June 1942.
———— "Technology, Utilization, and Productivity," *Bulletin de l'Institut International de Statistique,* 28th session, XXXIV, no. 4.
Steindl, J. *Small and Big Business — Economic Problems of the Size of Firms.* Oxford, 1945.

Stigler, G. "The Kinky Oligopoly Demand Curve and Rigid Prices," *Journal of Political Economy*, no. 5 (1947).

―― "Monopoly and Oligopoly by Merger," *American Economic Review*, Supplement, May 1950.

―― "The Statistics of Monopoly and Merger," *Journal of Political Economy*, no. 1 (1940).

Stigler, G., and K. E. Boulding, eds. *Readings in Price Theory*. London, 1953.

Sweezy, P. M. "Demand under Conditions of Oligopoly," *Journal of Political Economy*, no. 4 (1939).

Svennilson, I. *Growth and Stagnation in the European Economy*. United Nations Economic Commission for Europe. Geneva, 1954.

Sylos-Labini, P. "Monopoli, ristagno economico e politica keynesiana," *Economia internazionale*, November 1954.

―― "Il problema dello sviluppo economico in Marx ed in Schumpeter," in *Teoria e politica dello sviluppo economico*, ed. G. U. Papi. Milan, 1954.

―― "Relative Prices and Development Programmes," *Banca del Lavoro Quarterly Review* (Rome), September 1957.

Sylos-Labini, P., and G. Guarino. *L'industria petrolifera negli Stati Uniti, nel Canadà e nel Messico*. Milan, 1956.

Talamona, M. "Teoria dell'organizzazione, analisi microeconomica e teoria dell'oligopolio," *L'industria*, no. 2 (1961).

Tarshis, L. "The Flow of Business Funds, Consumption and Investment," in *Post-Keynesian Economics*, ed. K. K. Kurihara. New Brunswick, 1954.

Thorp, W. L., and W. F. Crowder. *The Structure of Industry*. Temporary National Economic Committee, Monograph No. 27. Washington, 1940.

Triffin, R. *Monopolistic Competition and General Equilibrium Theory*. Cambridge, Mass., 1940.

Tsiang, S. *The Variations of Real Wages and Profit Margins in Relation to the Trade Cycle*. London, 1947.

United Nations. *The Economic Development of Latin America*. Lake Success, 1950.

United States Department of Commerce. *Historical Statistics of the United States, 1790–1944*. Washington, 1945.

Whitman, R. H. "A Note on the Concept of 'Degree of Monopoly,'" *Economic Journal*, September 1941.

Wicksell, Knut. *Lectures on Political Economy*, trans. E. Classen and ed. L. Robbins. London, 1934.

Wilcox, D. "On the Alleged Ubiquity of Oligopoly," *American Economic Review*, Supplement, March 1950.

Willers, R. *The Dynamics of Industrial Management*. New York, 1954.

Wolfe, T. N. "The Problem of Oligopoly," *Review of Economic Studies*, no. 56 (1953–54).

Woytinsky, W. S. "Relationship between Consumers' Expenditures, Savings, and Disposable Incomes," *Review of Economics and Statistics*, no. 1 (1946).

———— "What Was Wrong in Forecasts of Postwar Depression?" *Journal of Political Economy*, no. 2 (1947).

Index

Administered prices, 73, 177
Advertising, 65–6
Agricultural products, "rich" and "poor," 110
Agriculture: and the multiplier, 172–3; competition in, 14, 71n; prices and incomes in, 104–5, 109–11; price supports, 109n, 139. *See also* Concentration; Parity ratio; Terms of trade
Andrews, P. W. S., 21, 31, 51
"Artificial" obstacles to entry, 2, 44, 53n23, 90, 131, 154
Automation, 135n

Backward countries, 36, 109n, 173–4, 185
Bain, J. S., 31–2, 85
Banking policy. *See* Credit policy
Bankruptcies, 149, 159
Blair, J. M., 73n
Breakeven point, 22n10
Breglia, A.: technological discontinuities, 36; entry and market form, 52; "monetary authority," 164
Business cycle. *See* Costing margin; Investment; Prosperity; Schumpeter

Capacity, unutilized, 41–2
Capital goods. *See* Machines; Producer goods
Capitalization of extraordinary profits, 90–3
Capital/output ratio, 62n, 149n
Chain stores, 15, 53
Chamberlin, E. H., 13n26, 15, 24, 33
Clark, C., 151
Compensation, theory of, 114
Competition: classical, 52–3, 103–6, 125–7, 153; neoclassical (or perfect), 52–3, 71n, 153; monopolistic, 12, 69, 90, 164; quality, 65–6. *See also* Product differentiation; Cost reductions
Concentration: absolute and relative, 8, 39; and market form, 8–11; in agriculture, 8n, 109n; in banking, 164; in commerce, 15, 53; in industry, 1–3, 109n; ratio, 5–8, 191–4; technical, economic, financial, 4, 6
"Conjectural variations," 19–20, 32, 34
Consumer goods, 55n, 69, 136–7
Corporations, 90–1, 139n17
Cost: direct or variable, 26–9, 40, 71, 86; fixed, 22, 41–2, 58, 71–2, 87; marginal, 26–9, 71n; reductions, consequences of, 63–4, 89, 93–4, 103–6, 122–9, 144, 154
"Cost of the struggle" (price wars), 45, 48–9, 64, 91
Costing margin, 31, 78; variations in, during the business cycle, 67–74, 96–7
Cournot, A., 19
Credit policy, 134, 164–6

Deficit spending, 184
Degree of monopoly. *See* Monopoly
Demand: and market form, 160–2; composition of, 161; expansion of, and entry, 61–2, 161; general, 33; special, 33, 69–70. *See also* Elasticity of demand; Exports, Investment; Public expenditure
Demand curve, 81; kinked, 20–5, 98; long-period, 31, 34; short-period, 31; shifts of, 34, 58, 61, 67, 69, 145
Depreciation, 28, 58, 85, 151. *See also* Investment
Depression, variations of direct cost and prices during, 69–74, 97–9

Development, economic: and diminishing returns, 133; conditioned by expansion of effective demand, 137, 145, 167–9

Differentiated oligopoly. *See* Oligopoly

Diminishing returns, 27, 104, 133, 174

Discontinuities, technological, 35–6, 54, 64, 81, 147, 174

Distribution of national income: changes in, 107–8; Kalecki's theorem, 84–8

Dynamic analysis, 137, 141

Economies: internal, 144; of scale, 29, 35, 62–3, 144n2, 194

Edgeworth, F. Y., 19

Elasticity of demand, 23, 34, 37, 44n, 51, 68, 78–80, 87, 146; arc, 37; empirical, 37–8; variations in, 63, 69–70, 73, 75

Elimination price. *See* Price

Employment. *See* Investment; Machines; Technical progress; Unemployment

Entry: of established firms, 61, 72–3, 147; of new firms, 43, 67, 149

Entry-preventing price. *See* Price

Equilibrium. *See* Price; Unemployment

European Common Market, 63n

Evely, R., 3n4, 5n6

Exports, 169

Fanno, M., 138n12, 164n9

Fellner, W., 177–8

Flexibility of prices and wages. *See* Price; Unemployment

Full-cost principle: 21–4, 57–8, 130; first and second criteria, 59–60, 75, 83

Galbraith, J. K., 19, 68n, 69, 73n

Garbarino, J. W., 98

Giles, B. D., 111

Gini, C., 5–6, 8, 191–4 (Appendix)

Good will of firms, 91

Gordon, R. A., 34

Great Britain: unemployment, 1850–1914, 138; investment in the 1930s, 151

Haberler, G., 95n, 163n7

Hall, R. L., 20–5, 31

Hansen, A. H., 151, 170–1, 175, 180, 182, 184, 186

Harrod, R. F., 24n15, 31, 69, 91

Hitch, C. J., 20–5, 31

Hoarding, 122–3, 152, 168

Imperfect oligopoly. *See* Oligopoly

Indifference curves, 35

Inflation, 107n, 173–5

Innovations, 63, 133–4, 143–4, 147–52, 171, 177; and replacement, 150; and investment, 143, 149; major, 63, 145–9, 167–8; minor, 144. *See also* Depreciation; Replacement

Integration: horizontal, 5; vertical, 5, 76

Interest, rate of, 134, 164–6

Interlocking directorates, 4

Inventories, cost of keeping, 165

Investment: and effective demand, 164–9; and employment, 133–42, 150–2, 161, 166–9; decisions, 159–162; financing of, and depreciation funds, 149, 168; incentives, 144–5; opportunities, 143–4, 170–1, 179, 186; replacement, 65, 135, 139, 150–1, 171. *See also* Investment; Replacement; Self-financing

Kahn, A. E., 161, 162n5

Kahn, R. F., 172, 176, 178n13

Kaldor, N., 13, 34, 36, 87–8

Kalecki, M., 77n, 84–8, 97n, 110n, 124, 186

Keynes, J. M.: "banana case," 123; relation between investment and employment, 133–6; technological unemployment, 134; economic stagnation, 138, 170; unemployment equilibrium, 140–2, 169–70; saving, 163–4, 179, 186; rate of interest, 165; public spending, 169, 171–6, 184

Kinked demand curve. *See* Demand curve

Lange, O., 130n, 146n4

Leontief, W., 80, 119

Lerner, A. P., 95
Levy, H.: process of concentration in modern industry, 1-3; technological discontinuities, 36
Linear programming, 35
Little, I. M. D., 3n, 5n6
Lombardini, S., 24n19, 55, 146n3
Lorenz curve, 5

Machines: changes in efficiency of, 65-6, 135-6; consequences of the introduction of, 112-29. *See also* Investment; Ricardo; Wicksell
Machlup, F., 24, 87n12
Macroeconomic and microeconomic analysis, 186-7
Marginal analysis, 23-5, 80-5; and oligopoly, 82; and monopoly, 51n16, 81-2
Marginal cost. *See* Cost
Market: form, 8-11, 155, 186; shares, 62, 83; size, 37, 46, 50, 56, 61-2
Markup. *See* Costing margin
Marshall, A.: trusts and monopolies, 10-12; prime cost, 27n; theory of the firm, 71-2; watering of stock, 93n; internal economies, 144
Marx, K., 9, 11, 115, 118, 135
Mason, E. S., 4, 70n13, 95n
Mergers, 7, 162
Modigliani, F., 43n, 51n17, 140
Monetary policy, 134, 164, 177. *See also* Credit policy
Monopoly, 51, 72, 82, 105; degree of, 6-7, 30, 53-4, 77n, 84-8, 95-6, 111
Multiplier, 167, 172-4

Obsolescence, 149, 150
Oligopoly: concentrated, 13, 15, 39, 55, 59-60, 69, 72, 94, 155; differentiated (or imperfect), 12, 15, 23, 53-5, 58-60, 65, 69, 70-2, 155; mixed, 14, 55; and competition, 51-2. *See also* Price; Product differentiation
Oligopsony, 74-6, 130n
Output, quantity changes in, 43-4, 46-7, 179
Overcapitalization, 91-3

Pareto, V., 35
Parity ratio, 109n
Patents, 56, 64
Patinkin, D., 141
Population growth, 167, 171, 178
Price: determination, 33-5, 50; entry-preventing, 40, 50; elimination, 40, 71; leadership, 39, 59-60; of machines, 50; of raw materials, 75-7, 87, 94; of variable factors, 50, 58-60, 67-77, 93-4, 97-8; trend, during the past century, 107n, 159; variations, 57-77
Price rigidity: long-run, 106-7, 129-31, 154; short-run, 94-9
"Privileged" firms and industries, 107-11
Producer goods, 55n25, 70, 136-7
Product differentiation, 5, 54-5, 65, 155
Profit: above-normal, 52, 103, 122, 125-6; maximization, 42n, 44n, 51, 68, 82-3; minimum rate of, 39-40, 42, 59; satisfactory level of, 83-4; undistributed, 152; unit, 89-91. *See also* Self-financing
Prosperity, variations of direct cost and prices during, 67-9, 96-7
Protectionism, 2, 53n22, 104, 131, 154n17
Psychological assumptions: and Keynesian theory, 163, 186-7; and theory of oligopoly, 19-20. *See also* "Conjectural variations"; Saving
Public expenditure: and economic stagnation, 171; productivity of, 173-7. *See also* United States.

Raw materials. *See* Price
"Reaction curves." *See* "Conjectural variations"
"Recession with inflation," 73n, 150
Replacement, 135, 139. *See also* Investment
Retail trade, and differentiated oligopoly, 14-15, 53
Ricardo, D.: competition and technical progress, 103-4; introduction of machinery, 112-18; relations between investment and employment,

133, 136–40; accumulation, 103, 160; role of demand, 160
Rigidity. *See* Price rigidity; Unemployment
Risk, 124
Robinson, J., 12, 15, 20n6, 24, 28n28, 106n10, 128n, 186
Rosenstein-Rodan, P. N., 36, 38, 149n9, 174
Ruggles, R., 77n, 95–7

Samuelson, P. A., 181
Saving: corporate, 163–4; excessive, 162–4; institutionalized, 163, 170; personal, 163–4, 179; public, 163; and psychological motives, 163, 179, 186
Schumpeter, J. A.: competition and large firms, 11, 152–3; oligopoly, 19, 130n; innovations, 63, 134–5, 143; demand elasticity in depression, 69–70; price flexibility, 105–6; development and growth, 133n; business-cycle theory, 138n12, 139n17, 147–9
Self-financing, 124, 153–5, 162, 166
Selling costs, "installation," 54–6
Services, 179
Shares, preferential and scrip issue of, 90–1
Singer, H. W., 109n
Size of firms, 38–9
Smith, A., 8, 11, 103–5, 133, 136
Sraffa, P., 10–12, 54n, 71n, 186
Stagnation, economic, 140, 170–2. *See also* Development; Public expenditure
Static analysis, 82, 85, 140
Stigler, G., 7n15, 92n, 98–9
Structure of industry, 33, 36–7, 41, 46–9, 79–80
Subsidiary activities, 2, 55n25
Supply curve: long-run, 29, 39, 144; short-run, 27–8
Sweezy, P. M., 20, 22, 25–6, 34, 186

Target-return pricing, 59n
Tarshis, L., 162n6, 163n8
Tax policy, 169
Tax reduction, 178, 184
Technical progress: and large firms,

64, 89, 105, 152; distribution of the fruits of, in competition and oligopoly, 103–11, 127–9, 152–3; effects on income and employment, 126–9, 140–2, 145. *See also* Innovations
Technology: and the equilibrium price, 38, 50; changes in, 63–4, 134–5. *See also* Discontinuities
Terms of trade: between agricultural and industrial products, 109–11, 139n15; between raw materials and industrial products, 109n
Trade. *See* Chain stores; Concentration; Exports; Retail trade
Trade unions, 68–9, 76, 93–4, 105, 111, 128n, 169
Transfer payments, 180
"Trustified capitalism," 141, 148
Tsiang, S., 77n, 95–7

Underdeveloped countries. *See* Backward countries
Unemployment: and flexibility of wages, 115–18, 141, 168; cyclical, 137–40, 175; frictional, 178; structural, 36, 173–4; technological, 133–4
Unemployment equilibrium, 140–2, 152, 169–70, 173–4
United States: agriculture, 139, 178–9; industrial concentration, 191–4; investment in the 1930s, 151; national product, 178, 180; public expenditure, 177–86; structure of employment, 179; unemployment, 138, 178

Vertical integration. *See* Integration
"Vicious circle" in investment and demand, 168–9, 179

Wages: during depression, 75–6, 94, 97–8; during prosperity, 68; share in national income, 85–7; trend of, 93–4, 104. *See also* Unemployment
Walras, L., 36
Welfare economics, 85n4, 154n18
Wicksell, K.: imperfect competition, 14–15; introduction of machinery, 115–18; monetary policy, 164–5